VILI A
RC

A HISTORY OF CHARLESTONE
UP TO THE TWENTIETH CENTURY

To Jeanne
With best wishes
Margaret

MARGARET FORREST took a degree in modern languages in 1950 at the University of London. She taught French and German at a Berkshire comprehensive during the 1960's. She came to live in Harlestone in 1990 and qualified as a Blue Badge Guide for Northamptonshire which aroused an interest in local history. This lead to a degree in Historical Studies in 2000 at Leicester University.

First published in Great Britain by Margaret Forrest

A CIP catalogue record for this book is available from the British Library

ISBN 978-0-9566218-0-1

Printed and bound by The Manson Group Ltd

Cover image(front): Original drawing of Harlestone House by the Repton Brothers courtesy of the Northamptonshire Record Office, Ref p182.
Cover image(reverse): page from the Estate Book of Henry de Bray

Contents

INTRODUCTION   IV

CHAPTER 1   **In the beginning**   7
             The Romans, The Anglo Saxons and the Danes,
             The Normans, After The Conquest

CHAPTER 2   **Manor Farm**   17
             The Mill, The Lumleys, The Bulmers, St Andrew's
             Church, Henry de Bray's Harlestone, Open Fields

CHAPTER 3   **The Village Takes Shape**   31
             The Quarries, The Reformation

CHAPTER 4   **The Sixteenth Century Village**   37
             The Civil War

CHAPTER 5   **Seventeenth Century Life**   41
             The Andrew Family

CHAPTER 6   **The Eighteenth Century**   49
             Harlestone Park, A New Road System, John Clend
             on's Tithe Book, Harlestone School, Enclosures,
             Sir Salathiel Lovell, Harlestone House, The Spencers

CHAPTER 7   **The Nineteenth Century Village**   67
             The Baptist Chapel

CHAPTER 8   **Loose Ends**   77

INDEX   80

APPENDIX 1   **The de Bray Family**   84

APPENDIX 2   **The Lumley/Bulmer Families**   85

APPENDIX 3   **The Camfield/Cooch Connection**   86

Harlestone Parish

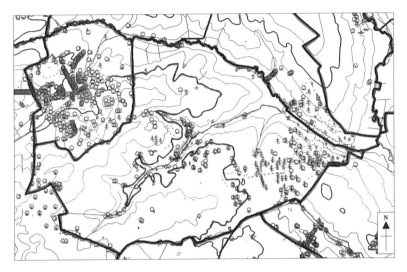

This map shows only natural features. The thick red line shows the parish boundaries. The thin red line is the 50ft contour. A comparison with a modern map shows how the village developed along the lines of the brook.

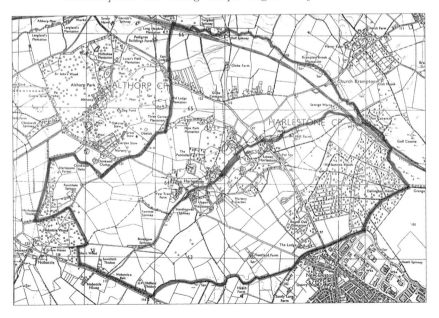

INTRODUCTION

Until two centuries ago, the basic building block of English society was the village. 95% of the population was engaged in agriculture, and the towns, closely linked to their agricultural hinterland, were, with few exceptions, little more than overgrown villages. Today the situation is reversed. 95% of the population is urban. Even people who work on the land are often forced by house prices to live in nearby suburbs. Villages are rapidly becoming either agreeable dormitories for well-heeled commuters, or the holiday resorts of occasional visitors. Before its original function disappears completely it is a good moment at which to look back at the history of one village – Harlestone, Northamptonshire.

Northamptonshire is a curiously lozenge shaped county which lies across the middle of England, approximately 70 miles north of London. Geologically speaking, and in broad terms, the northern and western part of the county is lias clay, and the southern and eastern part limestone, with considerable ironstone deposits. Through the middle runs a band of sandstone. The great glaciers, as they advanced and retreated, rounded off the little hills, and left in the valley of the Nene large deposits of sand and gravel. Harlestone lies on a stretch of Northampton Sand which provides the distinctive building stone of the village. It has a large variety of soils, ranging from sand to heavy clay. In his History of Northamptonshire, written in 1822, Baker describes the soil as 'extremely various, including woodland, light red land white loam and clay. The heath which is enclosed and planted with firs in ridings, spontaneously produces heath, fern and furze'. This is still largely the case.

The parish, lying four miles to the north and slightly to the west of the county town of Northampton, is bisected by Harlestone Brook, flowing from west to east to join Brampton Brook, which is in its turn a tributary of the Nene. The parish boundaries, originally defining to which church tithes should be paid, were settled at some time before 1086, when there is the first documentary evidence of a church.

Because of its springs of pure water, and many other natural advantages, the area has been a site of human settlement for many millennia, and traces of this long history are visible on the landscape, in the artefacts found on various sites, and in the documents which survive. Until the twentieth century it was an agricultural community. During that century many changes - the advent of mechanisation in agriculture, the revolution in communications, and the impact of two world wars - transformed the village. This study deals only with the earlier centuries, and leaves the village at the point at which the transformation to a modern community had gone beyond the point of no return.

1   IN THE BEGINNING

The only fossil remains recorded in Harlestone are those mentioned in a note in Baker's History of Northamptonshire, where he relates that "...the Reverend Mr. Shortgrave of Halston tells me that, about twenty years since, certain bones appearing to be those of some land animal were found included in the middle of a stone in Halston quarry and presented to the publick repository at Gresham College. I have searched that repository but could find nothing of them there..." The Reverend Shortgrave was Rector of this parish from 1682 to 1710, and the name of the village was at that time pronounced Halston or Alston. The gift to Gresham College has never been traced.

Almost as soon as the first farmers arrived in this island, this attractive valley was inhabited. There was a considerable prehistoric settlement on the slope running down from the Brampton Road to Harlestone Brook. Lines and circles, today only visible from the air, are probably signs of housing and agricultural enclosures, associated with quite sophisticated stock rearing, principally of sheep. A path connecting this settlement with the larger and more important settlement in the Bramptons, which became the backbone of the later village, can be traced today, continuing down Church Lane, following the brook to connect with what is now a dead end near the Post Office, and from there along the modern footpath across the Brington Road, up the lane opposite, and then along the footpath to reach the Roman Road.

Aerial Photograph South of the Brampton Road

Worked flints have been found in several places, mostly on the Heath. This was then a much larger swathe all round what later became the parish. Linear ditches and cropmarks, also mainly visible from the air, are other signs of this prehistoric occupation. Bridges, in his History of Northamptonshire, published in 1791, (though the evidence must date from before 1724, when Bridges died) states: "On a place called Dive's-heath are the remains of a fortification where human sculls and bones have often been dug up." All that now remains is a mound which has never been properly excavated, but it is likely to have been a prehistoric barrow or grave mound. There is also anecdotal evidence of post-holes and oyster shells seen during excavation work carried out in the 1940s to improve drainage in the farmyard of Park Farm, but these are now deeply buried under the concrete of later developments.

The last invaders before the Romans were Iron Age Celtic tribes. Northamptonshire was in the kingdom of the Catuvellauni. There is little direct evidence of their presence in the parish, except for traces in some of the outlying fields of Fleetland farm, but since there are Iron Age sites in nearby Duston and in Holdenby, it is likely that this valley too was peopled at that time. Fieldwork in the area is still ongoing, and may well produce more concrete evidence.

The Romans

It was in 43 AD that the Romans invaded England with a professional army, and colonised extensively in Northamptonshire. Watling Street, the major road which connected the coast and London with Chester and the north-west, and Ermine Street, the main road from the coast to the north-east, both run through Northamptonshire, and many Roman towns grew up in the area. Near Harlestone are Towcester and Bannaventa (east of Daventry) both on Watling Street, and, principally, Duston, only two miles away, where today a patchily excavated Romanobritish town lies under modern developments.

In Harlestone, there are four listed sites where significant Roman material has been found. New sites continue to be found by field-walkers; for instance, close to the ancient pathway to Harpole there are strong indications of a possible farmstead. The only site to be excavated so far has revealed the presence of a Roman villa. During the winter of 1927 and 1928, the Rector of the neighbouring parish of Great Brington, the Revd. H. O. Cavalier, carried out excavations in the field called Sharaoh (pronounced to rhyme with pharaoh) not far from the Roman road from Duston to Bannaventa. His methods were primitive, and would shock modern archaeologists, but he unearthed much that is of interest, though the villa may well be much more extensive than his limited excavations show. Every year, field walkers are still able to pick up pieces of Roman roof tiles, and some large pieces of carved stone lie in the nearby hedges.

The evidence of the pottery found on the site is that it was occupied from the mid Second Century onwards. However, the most interesting of his discoveries was that of a hoard of 814 Roman coins, close to a strangely hinged stone, which may have been a wall safe. The latest of these coins, which are now in the British Museum, dates from 395AD. That such a large sum was apparently abandoned, coupled with the discovery of burnt and broken roof timbers on the site, strongly suggests that the villa was destroyed and abandoned in the fourth or fifth century, possibly when the inhabitants fled before invading Anglo-Saxons. There were some indications that there had been squatters in the building at a later date, which again accords with the not uncommon practice of Anglo-Saxon invaders, who disliked stone buildings and tended merely to camp out in Roman ruins.

The Revd. H. O. Cavalier also found evidence of a hypocaust, and flue. Apart from the possibility that a more extensive layout may yet be found, a hint that the building may be of greater importance than a simple farmstead is in the foundations which were unearthed.

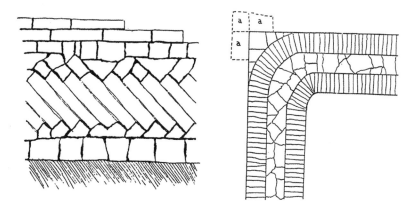

The drawing on the left shows the construction of the wall, with heavy slabs of stone, 18" long, 11" wide and 4" thick, laid at an angle on stones strongly bedded in mortar, with large stones laid on top. The illustration on the right shows the same wall from above, showing how cleverly the masons turned the corner. The explanation which the Revd Cavalier gave was that the clay soil made such a construction necessary, but it does seem remarkably sophisticated for a simple farmhouse.

The other three listed sites where there is evidence of Roman occupation, largely pottery shards, are much less rewarding, most probably because none has been properly excavated. One is at Church Farm, the two others in the fields near the road from Duston. At one of the sites near the Duston road, signs of slag were found, which seems to indicate some iron-smelting. If this is the case, then the development of the possibly prehistoric Port Road by the Romans to give it its present straight section, would be logical. Traces of the Romans continue to be found by accidental digging, for example, a coin was recently found in a garden in Upper Harlestone.

The Roman occupation brought some improvement in farming methods, with a heavier plough and stone barns. They introduced rabbits and the domestic cat, and some new crops, such as cultivated apples and pears, asparagus and sweet chestnut. The sweet chestnut trees which are a feature of the land to the west of the golf course, are ultimately descended from Roman stock. They also laid down a very extensive and well surfaced road system which endured well into the modern age. Watling Street runs close to Harlestone, and the road from Duston to Bannaventa, near Daventry which forms the western boundary of the parish is also Roman.

The ancient clapper bridge over the brook at the ford may also be of Roman origin. Another scholar has suggested that this is the bridge over which King Paeda, the son of King Penda, the last pagan king in England, marched on his way to

Peterborough c. 656, to build the first church on the site of the present cathedral. By the fourth century Roman urban society was already in decline, and Duston was abandoned. In 410 A.D. the last Roman legions were withdrawn from England.

Anglo-Saxons and Danes

Where the Romans left signs of their occupation in the villa and in the road system, there is much less evidence in Harlestone of the long centuries of Germanic presence. It seems likely that the native Romano-British inhabitants were slowly displaced over several centuries, and that the newcomers, being themselves farmers, took over existing farmsteads. Some of the field names give clues. 'Sharoah' deries from Old English 'schearu' a division, and 'horsemoor' from 'aust' = east. It is unlikely that this fertile valley was not exploited, since, according to the Victoria County History, most Anglo-Saxon settlements in Northamptonshire are where Northampton sand is close to clay formations, an exact description of Harlestone. However, only in the area of Glebe Lane near the northern border of the parish has significant material been found. Two loom weights, and two blackened hearthstones were found during the building of a house. This is the only place in the parish where there was any extensive house-building in the twentieth century, and therefore the only place where such accidental discoveries could be made. But there may of course be other reasons. These may include a move away from the valley during the years of cold summers and colder wetter winters which followed the world-wide climate change starting in 535A.D, when there was a huge volcanic eruption in the Sunda Straits. This was probably followed by Bubonic Plague, when conditions in Europe encouraged the spread of rats. The ensuing famine and plague brought a sharp fall in population, and the consequent shrinking or abandonment of settlements. The population of England at the departure of the Romans is estimated at 6,000,000 but in the Domesday Book survey the number has shrunk to 2,000,000.

Central England was the land of the Middle Saxons, and Northamptonshire eventually became part of the Kingdom of Mercia. In the ninth century there were extensive Scandavian settlements in Eastern England, including Northamptonshire, and the frontier with the Anglo-Saxon kingdoms settled down more or less along the line of Watling Street, just to the west of Harlestone. The area of Danish influence on laws and customs was known as the Danelaw. Danish settlement here was less dense than further north, but local names show scattered Danish influence, Althorp and Holdenby being the obvious examples. The name of this village may be derived from that of a Dane called Herolve who took over an existing Anglo-Saxon 'tun' during the Danish occupation, though an alternative but less persuasive explanation is that it may be associated, as 'Erolve' with the Peverel manor in a later century.

The village was almost certainly sacked in 1035, when Viking invaders marched down Watling Street, and, entering the county at Lilbourne, passed through Whilton, Brington, Althorp and Harlestone and then between Dallington and Duston so that Edwin could join his brother Morcar at Northampton. The Victoria County History recounts that:

> *'Morkere's Northern followers dealt with the country about Northampton as if it had been the country of an enemy. They slew men, burned corn and houses, carried off cattle, and at last led captive several hundred prisoners, seemingly as slaves. The blow was so severe that it was remembered when one would have thought that that and all other lesser wrongs would have been forgotten in the general overthrow of England. Northamptonshire and the shires near it were for many winters the worse.'*

In Domesday Book in 1086 some lands in Harlestone are still recorded as 'waste', and one estate rose in value from 5 shillings in the time of Edward (1042-1066) to 30 shillings – a remarkable recovery in a short time, but also an indication of the extent of the devastation.

Before the Conquest there seem to have been three manors, one paying dues to the King through the Manorial Court of Upton, one possibly belonging to thanes in the soke of Fawsley, and one to Gitda, possibly the wife of Earl Ralf of Hereford, nephew of Edward the Confessor. The only names given in Domesday Book are Leuric, Orgar and Edric, who held as freeholders the land which was later given to the Count of Mortain. The village lay in the Nobottle Hundred, the Anglo-Saxon grouping for tax purposes.

This Scandinavian type society had its axis towards the North Sea, and the kingdom was broadly united under one rule of law, enforced by the shire reeve, with one national system of money and taxation – the only country in Europe to have such advanced administration. But the middle years of the century brought disruption. After the death of Edward the Confessor, there were many disputes about the succession, eventually settled by Duke William of Normandy, who invaded in 1066.

The Normans

The invasion was strongly resisted, and to enforce their domination, the Normans built castles all over the country. Waltheof, Earl of Northampton, at first made peace with William, but in 1072 he joined a failed rebellion, and was executed. William then put one of his own henchmen, Simon de Senlis, in charge of the area. Simon replaced the motte and bailey castle which had been built in Northampton after the conquest in 1068 with a more permanent stone structure. This was one of the largest urban castles in England, and its construction must have absorbed a huge work force. It is more than likely that people from neighbouring villages - we must suppose including Harlestone - were involved in such a massive task. It seems likely that when Simon de Senlis went off to the First Crusade in 1086, he was accompanied by at least one man from Harlestone. In 1888 when soil was being removed from the wall of the Rectory stables, just outside the churchyard, the discovery was made of an Arabic gold coin struck by the Khalif El Mansoor in A.D. 768 The most probable explanation is that it was buried with a returning crusader in the late eleventh or early twelfth century.

After the Conquest

Harlestone began to assume much the shape it is today, with the church at the point where the track over the brook crossed the ancient track from the Bramptons. The chief landowners were the heirs of the two major tenants-in-chief of the Conqueror, his half brother the Count of Mortain and William Peverel. The king kept for himself the land held by his predecessors through the manor of Upton, about 60 acres. 15 of these acres were given to the Abbey of St. James, which lay on the outskirts of Northampton, not far from Harlestone. This abbey, founded c. 1104 on the north side of the town, was a house of the Augustinian Canons, and very well reputed. The name recurs in the later history of the village, and it often received charitable gifts of land and money from people in Harlestone. Of the remaining royal land holdings, 21 acres eventually came into the hands of the de Bray family, and the rest remained in the hands of freemen.

But now the feudal system, where all lands belonged to the King, and were held in return for knight service, was in force. There was a seismic change in English society. All senior posts in the church were filled by Normans. The French language replaced Anglo-Saxon at court and among the Norman rulers. Latin remained the language of the church and of the law, but English was the language of ordinary people. It took several centuries for these two traditions to fuse together to make one nation.

Much of the land in the main estates was leased or rented. Some of the rents demanded are curious to modern eyes. Half a yardland was rented for a pair of white gloves annually (or 1 penny - a measure of the value of the gloves). The Abbey of St. James demanded a pound of cumin annually from a tenant oddly also called Cumin, (did he possibly specialise in the preparation of these aromatic seeds?) and this thirteenth century charter specifies that the rent in cumin should be appropriated only to the maintenance of the infirm at St. James's. Robert, Prior of Dallington, grants a yardland for a pound of pepper or six pence annually, and Hingerain Cumin rents half a yardland for 5 marks silver, instead of a pound of cumin annually, an indication of the values attached to flavouring herbs and spices. In 1363 land was rented for a rose for the first thirteen years and then 20s per annum. Some other important rights were granted and regulated by charters; Robert Glazun got by charter the right to cut peat annually for half a day by one man on the heath of Harlestone, showing that this fuel was used here as well as wood. The manorial courts oversaw all these arrangements.

William Peverel in 1117 founded the Priory of Lenton near Nottingham, and as part of its endowment gave it the advowson, or right to appoint priests and to take a share of the tithes, of the church of St. Andrew, Harlestone. The priory exercised this right until the Reformation. Those lands in Harlestone given to William Peverel came later into the hands of the Earls of Derby, and a certain Brixtan de Armenters was their tenant in the late twelfth century. His daughter Quena, who was a minor when he died, married without the consent of the Earl, who then confiscated her inheritance, and gave it to William de Staunton. Quena's daughter, Emma, married a man called Henry de Bray. Their grandson built Manor Farm, still standing in the village.

A.—Dove House (probably rebuilt).
B.—Sloping ground leading to covered-in Ponds and Stream.
C.—Spring (modern well).

D.—Old Kitchen.
E.—Modern additions.
F.—Part of old Roof and Walls.
G.—Old Granary.

I.—Site of Hall pulled down about 1902 (probably Henry de Bray's 'aula').
J.—Site of Bakehouse pulled down about 1895.
K.—Disused Quarries.
H.—Old Barn.

REMAINS OF HENRY DE BRAY'S BUILDINGS AT HARLESTONE.

16

2   MANOR FARM

All the information about the building of Manor farm comes from an account that Henry de Bray, great-grandson of Quena, kept from around 1330. This manuscript, known as the Estate Book of Henry de Bray, is now in the British Museum, and is an invaluable record of life in Harlestone in the early fourteenth century. It is principally the record of the legal arrangements by which his father and grandfather had recovered through the manorial courts the lands taken from Quena. He appears to have kept it to protect his daughter, and sole heiress, from the de Staunton family. It is written in Latin, the lingua franca of scholarship at the time, with interpolations in both French and English, both languages still being in common use – French in the ruling classes, and English for the others.

First in A.D. 1289 Henry built a hall with a chamber at the north end, which cost £12 apart from stone and timbers. The stone came from quarries close to the site of the house – the 'hills and hollows' which are now a playground for local children.

In 1291 he added a chamber at the south end of the hall, costing £5 10s. A note states that all the timbers for the chamber grew in his courtyard. During the following years he made many improvements to the property. In 1297 he added a pigsty and henhouse 'with walls towards the east up to the oxstall' for 56s; in 1301 a new barn which cost £15 2s; in 1304 a new granary for £4 12d. and a new sheepfold for 20s.and a small house to hold the carts. In 1303 he added a new kitchen, which cost 40s., including a 'fountain' nearby for greater convenience. All these buildings were whitewashed.

Of the two barns he built, one stood where there is now an orchard, and was only demolished in the nineteenth century

The main part of the house has been replaced and modernised over the centuries, but the chamber at the south end of the hall, which has become a barn, still has the original gables and buttresses from the fourteenth century.

In 1293 he made fishponds below the house, and these hollows can still be detected. In 1302 he made a "mound" in the court near the Saltwell. This mound was probably an earthen mound built as a seat against the wall, and covered with turf. A garden seat of this type can be seen in the reconstructed medieval garden at the Prebendal Manor in Nassington, Northamptonshire. A wall enclosed much of the land surrounding the house, a total length of 20 perches at a cost of 28s.

A few years later, in 1305, he added a dovehouse at the corner of the herb garden. The dovecote fell down only in the 1950s. The situation of the 'dovehouse,' in an agreeable and sweet-smelling part of the garden may well be as part of the pleasure gardens. This was not uncommon at the time.

Henry's barn c.1890

14th Century buttresses at Manor Farm

The dovecote at Manor Farm c.1950

The Mill

Apart from the house, Henry also built cottages on his land, and, another major investment, built and repaired both the watercourses leading to it and the watermill itself, a little way downstream from Manor Farm. Although a mill is mentioned in Domesday Book, there is reason to think that this is not the mill whose ruins still stand, but an earlier one which the Normans found when they seized the lands. In Domesday Book the lands given to the Count of Mortain include; 'a mill at two shillings'. The Count of Mortain's lands later became the Lumley Estate in Upper Harlestone, so it is unlikely that this is the mill whose ruins still lie in Lower Harlestone. Henry de Bray has a memorandum: "that in the time of Lord Ralph de Thenerchebray soldier there was a mill in le Bewe below my cultivated land which was called Old Milne Hul and to this belonged ditches and mill sites which later were torn away by the stream and carried away". This was probably the Domesday Book mill, likely to have been built of wood, and therefore easy to sweep away. He notes that in 1299 he spent £9 6s. 4d. 'in building a watermill in le Whetecroft where my ancestors had in olden times a mill and in the making of a millpond' which is certainly the mill whose ruins survive. The thick walls of the foundations indicate its Norman origin. It is this mill which Henry improved during his work

19

The Dovecote in Upper Harlestone

on Manor Farm.

One year later in 1300 he spent a further £4 13s. 4d, in repairing the water mill constructed in the preceding year. In subsequent years he repaired watercourses leading to the mill, and finally in 1308 built a bridge above the mill at a cost of ten shillings. This mill was for him a good investment and brought him in a good revenue. It was smaller than it later became, and had only one pair of stones. Later, the water wheel, which had been outside the building, was incorporated into an enlarged building, and in the nineteenth century it was converted to steam power. In the twentieth century, in spite of its picturesque location, it was allowed to fall into decay to the degree that, when the fashion for restoration began, repair was no longer possible.

Henry also mentions a windmill, which stood near the road called Windmill Hill. A mill on this site was still in use in the last century, and with another on the Heath, to which a track led over Dives Heath, was largely for animal feedstuffs.

The Lumleys

The 190 acres in Harlestone given to the Count of Mortain passed later to the de Keynes family. Under this family, it was in the twelfth century held by Hugh de Heyford, one of whose descendents, Agnes, married Hugh de Morwick, a northern knight. She had three daughters and coheiresses, Sibilla, Beatrice and Theophania. Sibilla married Sir Roger Lumley of County Durham, and had first her own inheritance, and then, when her sister Beatrice died without an heir, her share too. She had two sons. The elder, Robert, remained in the north, and his descendents became the Earls of Scarborough. There is still a Lumley Castle in County Durham. As his share of the inheritance, Robert gave the Harlestone lands to his younger brother Roger.

The descendents of Roger de Lumley lived in Harlestone until 1500. The name appears regularly in early legal documents. In 1316 Roger de Lumley was called 'Lord of Harleston' In 1364 Robert Lumley purchased Althorp, but his son John sold it again in 1414. John's brother Richard inherited the Harlestone estate, followed by his son Robert, who married Joan, daughter of Edmund Dyve of Brampton. Their son John was born 1450, but he had no children, and sold the estate to Thomas Andrew of Charwelton in 1500. John Lumley and his wife Alice were allowed to continue in the use of the property, since Thomas Andrew did not wish to live there.

The house they occupied was on, or near, the site of the present Dovecote House. It was a large house with extensive outbuildings. There were chambers above the great hall, and a large barn with stabling for six horses.

All that remains is the Dovecote. It has today has been much restored, and is in essence a fifteenth century building, but it is a reminder of the privileges enjoyed by Lords of the Manor in medieval times. There are nesting boxes for 200 birds, who could fly in and out through the overhanging eaves, providing winter food for their owners, and in later centuries saltpetre for making gunpowder from their droppings.

The Bulmers

The other heiress of Hugh de Morwick, Theophania, who inherited the third share of his property in Harlestone, married Ralph de Bulmer, also from the north, and her descendents held a third of the land known as the Manor of Harlestone until the fifteenth century. They also held lands in Heyford, Brington, Collingtree and Brockhall. Their presence in the village is difficult to trace, as is the possibility that they had a manor house somewhere here. The name recurs in documents over the next two centuries. Edward III gave the then rector of Harlestone, John Pykard de Carleton, the custody of a third part of the Bulmer estate, after the death of Ralph Bulmer, to hold until the legal age of his son and heir, possibly implying that the boy was resident in the parish. An agreement of 1410 about the division of the common fields has 'The Lord of Bolymer' as one of the signatories. That the Bulmer interest continued is shown in 1410 when the agreement about the fields was reached, and the document was signed by the lords with interests in the parish, i.e. the Abbot of St. James, Robert Lumley, the lord of the Bulmer share, John Lumley, Laurence Dyve, and William Coveley. (All, except for William Coveley, are familiar names from the twelfth century divisions of land.) Six freemen signed for the men and vill of Harlestone. Disputes were to be settled by a majority of nine men, seven named by the lords, and two representing the village. They agreed the sequence of lands left fallow, the use of meadow and pasture, and also the areas which the lords had enclosed 'to keep out the beasts of Harlestone men, but if they break in they will be impounded'. This agreement held for at least 100 years, as on the back are details of its being renewed in 1490, and in 1504, in each case by nine local men. But in 1441, Sir Ralph de Bulmer placed all his lands, including his estates in Harlestone, in the hands of trustees, who separately or together held the Bulmer lands, and the Bulmer share seems to disappear until the eighteenth century.

St Andrew's Church

Henry de Bray was also a leading figure in the rebuilding of St. Andrew's Church. In the Estate Book he tells us:

Master Richard De Het was rector likewise at the beginning of 1292, and he built the new chancel in 1320 and the same Richard was rector for 42 years. The whole church was made anew in the time of the said rector in the year 1325, Roger de Lumley procured the iron and smithy work, Henry de Bray the stone and timber, John Dyve the carpentry work.

Henry underlined his contribution to the parish by placing effigies of himself and his wife Mabel on either side of the inside of the South door, where they still survey the church they built. Richard de Hette lies in the chancel in front of the high altar. His grave slab was uncovered during Victorian restoration work, and replaced where it belonged, at a slightly higher level than it was originally. John Dyve was Henry's son-in-law, having married his only daughter, Alice, and Roger de Lumley was the Lord of the other manor in Harlestone.

There had been a church in Harlestone already for several hundred years. Indeed, it may well have been built on a site already sacred to a pagan diety. This was a common practice, and the spring under the floor of the cross-aisle of the nave is very suggestive. A church was certainly there in 1086 at the time of Domesday Book, and the circular shape of the churchyard which survives at the north-west corner seems to indicate its Anglo-Saxon origins. Harlestone is one of only four villages in the Nobottle Grove Hundred to have had a church at Domesday Book. There is no documentary evidence about this early church, though the roof line visible on the tower may be from that building. This would indicate that the earlier building was smaller than the present church, with a thatched roof. The tower dates from the twelfth century, and may well be from the time of William Peverel, who had given the advowson to the Priory of Lenton in 1107. Apart from the font, which is dated early thirteenth century, no other traces of this earlier church remain.

We also learn from the Estate Book that in 1294 an acre of land in Grindale was given to Richard de Hette by the 'commune of the vill' for sufficient income for bell ropes. This land was henceforth appropriately called Bellropes, and provided this service until the Reformation. The vill also contributed wax to the church (for the wax candles at the altar) at 3d per virgate (i.e. 30 acres) from 27 virgates of land.

Henry made a list of all the priests from 1227 until his death, most of whom would have lived beside the church. An updated list hangs today in the Church. It is reasonable to suppose that the first house on the site of the Rectory was quite a small priest's house, suitable for a celibate priesthood. The priest of the church of Harlestone held "one large place which lies between the cottage of Henry de Bray and the garden of Roger de Lumley next to the gate of the said Roger of the King's fee which lord Ralph de Thenerchebray gave to the church." He also had "half a virgate in the King's fee in the domain of the Abbey of St. James". This land he

St Andrew's Church

would have worked himself, for the support both of himself and of the church. In addition he had tithes of a tenth part of all produce in the parish. Such tithes had been enforceable by law since 960 A.D. It is likely that the oversight of the Priory of Lenton kept these lands and their income intact until the reformation, making Harlestone a wealthy living.

The church was also involved in the management of the common fields. The churchwardens appointed bird scarers, mole catchers, and so on, and had custody of the village plough. The church bells announced the start of agricultural operations which had to be carried out at the same time such as sowing, and reaping and also when gleaning might begin.

The bare stone walls of the present day give no indication of the rich colours and decoration in medieval times. Wall paintings, statues and altars of saints and stained glass windows brought colour and light into lives in which both housing and clothing were monochrome. Documented in wills of the period are altars and chapels to the Virgin Mary, Saint Anne and Saint Nicholas. Apart from the clerestorey, which was added at sometime during the sixteenth century, it remains an essentially fourteenth century church, much as Henry de Bray and his fellows built it.

Henry de Bray's Harlestone

Harlestone was then and for many centuries vitually a self-contained community. It was not isolated, having good connections to Northampton town and to neighbouring villages, but Henry's interest was essentially parochial. He makes passing references to the execution of Piers Galveston, the extinction of the order of Templars, and the hanging and quartering of the Despensers. A reflection of the tensions caused by the enmity between the Queen Isabella and her husband Edward II over his favourites. Otherwise there are few references to the outside world.

Almost everything the people used was provided locally. Food came from the crops and animals, and wood from the surrounding woods for furniture and tools and fuel. The heath provided additional fuel with peat and furze. The church looked after not only the spiritual needs of the parish, but also the care of the sick and indigent, and provided some education. St. James's Abbey was the chief local source of such assistance. Throughout the Estate Book, the pervasive presence of the Church is evident. Many dates are given as from various religious festivals, today very obscure – for example "from the feast of the purification of the Virgin" (February 2) until "the day after the Advincula of St. Peter" (August 1), "at the feast of the Exaltation of the Holy Cross" (September 16) "at the feast of St. Margaret the Virgin" (July 20) and "at the feast of St. Dunstan" (May 19). The rhythms of the church calendar were an essential part of normal life.

Justice was locally administered except for major crimes. The Estate book gives many details of the way in which justice was exercised. Manorial courts judged civil matters, relating to the working of the open fields, and the infringement of local bye-laws. Penalties mentioned in the Estate Book include fines for straying animals:

> *Item one stray sheep price 6d.*
> *Item one stray lamb price 3d.*
> *Item one stray beast of burden price 4s .*
> *Item one stray beast of burden price 10d.*
> *Item another stray beast of burden price 10d.*
> *Item one stray chicken price 2s. 4d.*

Notice that a higher value was placed on a stray chicken than on a stray sheep!

Other offences were :

> *'That John Berwell ploughed unlawfully above the King's way 3d.' and 'that Robert Sebod ploughed unlawfully over the King's Way'*

This was not difficult to do when roads were simple cart tracks, and it was a way in which a man sought to extend his land.

Also: *'that John Howet put dung on the King's way to the harm of all'.*

He was ordered to remove it under the penalty of 40d.

'Hue and cry' was raised against several people. This was a communal system of law enforcement, where neighbours could be called upon by the victim to help to pursue criminals. It was a legal obligation to help in this way. If the stolen goods were found on the arrested person, he could be summarily executed.

> *Agnes Lac raised the hue and cry against Henry - lawfully agreed.*
> *Item it was represented that William Irney raised hue-and-cry against John West lawfully, by the pledge of Henry Bust.*
> *Item Lucy Faber raised hue-and-cry against Alice Ekebriege by the pledge of William Irney.*

In addition, local magistrates had the duty of ale and bread tasting to maintain quality and purity of these basic foods. Water was generally not pure enough to drink and 'small beer' was the normal drink. There were many offences against the licensing laws.

That Henry Clerke brewed three times against the law 2d.
That because it was sold without the seal of the fee 1d.
That John brewed likewise against the assise 1d.
That Richard Gifford brewed against the assise 6d.
That Agnes Lac brewed for 3 years similarly every week.

Henry records that: 'William Grew surrenders the post of frankpledge and William Hessle is elected and makes his oath in Harleston.' Frankpledge was a system of law and order under which men were organised into groups of ten households, each responsible for the behaviour of its members. This does not seem to have been strictly observed. He mentions 30 elapsed years, for which fines were imposed, but they were 2d. and therefore very small. Even at the reconvened frankpledge court, several people were fined for non-appearance, so it was not taken very seriously.

Major issues were decided by the eyre, a circuit of royal judges instituted by Henry II to administer justice. At the Eyre of Northampton in 1329 judgement was made on a Harlestone crime when a quarrel between Elias Bokelard and John Bate, led to John killing Elias. He immediately sought sanctuary in St. Andrew's Church, where he confessed his crime and 'abjured the realm' i.e. fled the country. He had to carry a wooden cross, and to go to the named port of departure, never straying from the highway. If he did he could be killed. It is not recorded whether he made it to the port.

A dispute between Hugh de Staunton and the Priory of Lenton about the advowson of St. Andrew's also went to the Eyre of Northampton to be tried before the Lord Chief Justice. Curiously, Henry makes no mention of this affair in which his family must have been involved. It may have been recorded in the ten or so missing pages of the Estate Book. The incident took place in 1329, when the de Staunton family tried to claim the right to appoint the next rector. In the course of this family's disputes with the de Brays, they had already tried unsuccessfully to claim this right in 1279, but their claim was rejected by an ecclesiastical court. This time the matter was to be settled by Trial by Combat, oddly enough at the insistence of the Prior of Lenton. The judge, the Lord Chief Justice, did his best to get the parties to agree but to no avail, and lists were set up and the champions, armed and ready for the fight, appeared. At the very last moment, the Stauntons withdrew their claim, much to the annoyance of the Lord Chief Justice who was presiding. He accused them of wasting his time, the King's time, and the time of all the spectators, and made them run two demonstration jousts, and then to wrestle. Accounts of this event, which also contain precise descriptions of the armour the champions wore, and the preparations they made before the fight, are fully described in the records of the Eyre, indicating that it was a rare event, especially in church affairs, and worthy of note.

Henry farmed most of his lands himself, but also leased land to tenants. In 1329 he had 24 tenants, who paid him in rent in that year £9 15s. Farming was still on the open field system, which had been normal in England since before the Conquest, and which continued until the eighteenth century.

Open Fields

Open-field agriculture involves cooperative exploitation of all the land in a settlement. The smallest agricultural unit was the 'land', which was a strip usually about 220 yards in length, and the width a sower could conveniently strew, between a quarter and half an acre in extent. A group of lands lying together was known as a furlong. Furlongs were aligned as far as possible north and south, but also according to the aspect of the land, its fertility, and any natural features involved. A farm consisted of a number of scattered lands, usually about 80, lying in the common fields. Henry de Bray held no fewer than 111 strips. The parish was at that time divided into two fields, the North field and the South field, separated by Harlestone Brook. Fields or large sections of fields, were left fallow on a cycle of two, three or four years, and animals were pastured on the stubble after harvest or in the fallow year. Throughout this time, farming in Harlestone was mixed, with corn, rye and wheat being the main cereal crops, alternating with beans and peas, and sheep and cattle were the animals raised. Pigs roamed in the woodlands which surrounded the settlement. Temporary enclosures were made whenever animals had to be kept separate, perhaps for breeding purposes, but they were made of wattles and willows, and could be removed when wished.

The system evolved over the centuries to suit the needs of changing agricultural practices, becoming three fields in the fifteenth century by an agreement between men of the village and the six lords who then owned lands there. In the seventeenth century it seems to have beccome a five field system. It was ecologically a very sound system which kept the land in good heart for nearly one thousand years. It was organised round the church, where the churchwardens were responsible for appointments to those tasks which applied to all the farmers such as bird scarers, mole catchers and someone to keep animals off the cultivated fields. They ensured that seed time and harvest times were coordinated, and appointed officials like the hayward, who had charge of the fences and enclosures. The church bells sent

28

signals to workers in the fields such as the time when gleaning could start. Since the priests were also farmers, with the church owning nearly a hundred strips in the common fields - nearly as many as the largest lay landowners - there was a very close relationship between the church and the land. It was the eighteenth century before the system came to an end, when with enclosures and the end of tithing the link was broken.

3   THE VILLAGE TAKES SHAPE

Henry de Bray recorded an apparently stable society, but changes were coming which he could not foresee. From the twelfth until the middle of the fourteenth century the climate in England had been benign, giving good harvests, and relative prosperity, with an increase in population. Then the climate changed, and there was a long period of cold, wet weather. This brought failures of harvests and consequent famine, leaving the population open to disease. It is significant that one of the last entries in the Estate Book (written later than the other entries, and in another hand) is a recipe for a specific against the plague. Plague was recorded in the county frequently, the worst being the Black Death in 1349, when the population of England shrank from around 5 or 6 million people to 3 million. It is unlikely that Harlestone escaped. The addition of the porch to the church is believed to have been delayed by the Black Death.

The drop in population brought significant social changes. The feudal system, whereby tenants paid their overlords in days of labour, was brought to an end by the shortage of labour, and the labourers consequent new ability to bargain for better conditions. Harlestone would have been less affected than most. By this time the Dyve family had moved to Bedfordshire, the position of the Bulmers is unsure, and Robert Andrew was just starting on his acquisitions in the area, so only the Lumleys actually lived in the village. Many semi-independent small farms developed.

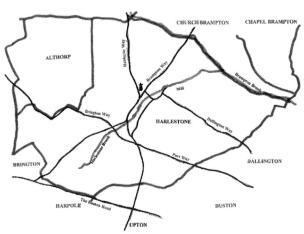

From the boundary markers to his fields that Henry names, the road system at his time can be reconstructed. The main road from Northampton diverged from the present A428 at Hopping Hill, and joined Port Road to go through Upper Harlestone. Henry mentions this road as a boundary marker called the King's Way. He also mentions Dallington Way, which today runs as a footpath through Harlestone Firs, and Holdenby Way, which has become a track over the fields from past the church. 'The way near the Saltwell' is probably the road to the ford. This was an important connector to the mill from the western part of the village, and to the pathway to Duston which ran along the southern side of the brook, and is still a footpath. All these tracks formed an intricate complex of pathways which served to unite all the vital services of the community.

When Henry de Bray died, c. 1340, Manor Farm was inherited by his only daughter, Alice, who had married John Dyve of Brampton in 1308. In the next century the Dyves lost their lands in Brampton, and in 1420 the family moved to Bedfordshire. They held on to the estate in Harlestone, which was leased or rented to tenants for the next two hundred years.

After the sale of their estate to Thomas Andrew in 1500, John Lumley and his wife Alice were allowed to live on in their manor house, since Thomas did not want to live there, but this branch of the family then died out. Another branch, possibly through a connection with a Brington Lumley, came back into the village in the sixteenth century. A document about the enclosure of some fields in 1517 for a man called Nicholas Kynne, includes the name of John Lumley, Knight, and the birth of Thomas Lumley, quarryman, in 1545 and his death in 1603 are recorded. Subsequently, many are mentioned as stoneworkers or quarrymen, but they were certainly not simple labourers.

The village by this time was a loose collection of farms united along the line of the brook and the path which followed it. There was a centre round the church, where the path over the ford crossed the main track. Cottages were grouped round the farms where the people worked, and they were at first largely of wood. One of the conditions Henry had laid down for the renewal of a lease was that the tenant should maintain the wood of the walls and the thatch of the cottage in good condition "as they are at present." Cob a mixture of straw and gravel, was also used but no houses of the type survive. A cottage which stood until 1940 near Mother Redcap's well close to the Heath was partly built of cob. It burnt down in farcical circumstances in 1940 when firemen could not get water from the brook and had to stand by to watch the house burning.

The Quarries

Because of the easy availability of stone, it slowly replaced cob and wood even for cottages. Harlestone quarries have long provided a source of alternative employ-

Harlestone quarry in the nineteenth century

ment in the village. Under a layer of turf and subsoil, which provides coarse small stones for roads or infillings, lie layers of sand. Beneath these are the layers of stone for buildings, and finally underneath everything is to be found soft 'cotter' used in later centuries by careful housewives for cleaning window sills and door steps. Near groups of houses, old quarries are clearly visible, from which the convenient stone was taken.

In Henry's time, the stone was quarried by peasants under their Lord's control. A man called William le Pewerel held land by villein tenure from Henry. (That is to say that he was bound to the land and essentially a serf) Because he had worked "long and diligently in my service and was faithful", Henry freed him and gave him and his wife Christine a house and land for 20 silver shillings at the usual four terms for all their lives with 'one bedrip and hedrip' for all feudal services (that is to say, service on the land at stated times) on condition that he would quarry all the stone for all buildings and walls Henry might build while he lived. This mixture of rent and service was typical of the contracts made at that time. Henry did not profit much from this agreement, for William Pewerel died in April 1303, but after his death the property descended to the eldest of his sons. It was probably this son who provided the stone for Henry's building projects, chiefly Manor Farm and the church.

In later centuries men worked in the quarries as alternative employment to farming, and stonemason had become a recognized trade. In 1535, John Stormer wills that his son 'shall occupie the delff after me and all such things that long to the said delff at the will of the Lord.' 'Delff' is an old word for the hollows made by quarrying. Even when it was quarried in Duston, the local stone was called Harlestone

stone. Such stone was used to build Kislingbury village, also much of Harpole and some of the larger houses in Milton Malsor. It was also used in many other churches and great houses in the county, largely because of its particularly attractive colour. In some quarries stone for slates was found. This is in two forms – a limestone which occurs in sections in different parts of the county, specifically in the Limekiln quarry on Hopping Hill, and in Northampton Sand at Duston and Harlestone Heath where it has been mined since at least 1712.

By the sixteenth century most people lived in stone houses, and many of the surviving cottages date from this time, but much modified over the centuries to meet changing needs. They started as simple one storey buildings with two rooms and possibly a loft under the thatched roof, then a second storey with sleeping accommodation was added in the upper storey. Windows in the upper floor were first on the gable wall, and then dormers were inserted into the thatched roof. Once fireplaces were no longer in the centre of the main dwelling room, chimneys allowed two rooms to be heated at once, and the large inglenook fireplace developed In individual houses this progression can often be traced, though more recent modernisations have often obscured or destroyed traces of earlier change.

The major farms were fine stone buildings. Most seem to be on sites of earlier buildings, and all are on good sources of water. Roman remains have been found at Church Farm. Rock Farm, with its very deep well, dates from the 14th century, though much altered in later centuries. The house at Yew Tree Farm dates from the eighteenth century, but the ancient yew has been dated to 1189, with a note that it was probably cut back in 1918, and was a sapling from an older stem. In the 1980s a stone quern was found here, which was probably Saxon but may even be of Roman origin. The spring there is particularly prolific. Park Farm was originally the Glebe farm, in close association with the church and the rectory.

Apart from plagues, national events do not seem to have affected the village until the sixteenth century.

The Reformation

When Henry VIII separated the church in England from the universal Catholic Church, one of his acts was to dissolve the monasteries. In 1534 the priory of Lenton fell victim, and as a result, Henry himself took the advowson of St. Andrew's into his own hands and he appointed – or had appointed - the next priest, Sir Nicholas Archbold. This priest stayed through the reign of Edward VI, which was the time when the major shift towards Protestantism occurred in the Church of England. It should be noted that the title 'Sir' does not indicate knighthood, but only that he was a secular priest, i.e. not belonging to one of the religious orders such as the Dominicans, Franciscans or Augustinians. (The title 'Master' indicates that the holder had a degree of Master of Arts, and 'clerk' that he was in minor orders or a deacon. Of the last six priests before the reformation, four were simply 'Master', and one was 'Sir'.) The advowson was then sold to Edward Lord Clinton and Sage, who granted it to George Tresham of London, and John Busshoppe of Northamptonshire, who in their turn sold it to Valentine Gregory of Harlestone in 1552.

Henry VIII's son Edward VI was a fanatical protestant, and during his short reign many churches were desecrated, and anything that smacked of Catholicism destroyed. In Harlestone, all the altars and chapels to the Virgin Mary, Saint Anne, Saint Nicholas, and the Rood Screen were destroyed, the stained glass windows broken, and the walls whitewashed. Today only a few scraps of green and red remain in the tracery of the windows. There must have been sufficient support in the village to let this destruction take place. Northampton town was a centre of dissenting thought, and it would be surprising if Harlestone was not to some degree affected by its larger neighbour. The only slight clue that it was not universally popular is shown in the legacy of Elizabeth Cocks in 1588, when she left money to the church 'for the buying of suche things as be most necessarie by the discrecion of the requirement there', which would seem to be to replace items destroyed earlier.

During the reign of Queen Elizabeth I the Anglican Church took its final form as an established, Episcopal church, outside the Roman communion. From then on, with the advent of the Bible in English and the Book of Common Prayer, the English church developed a character of its own, and the appointments of priests, and their role in the community began to change. The new dispensation seems to have been accepted in the village, on the evidence of surviving wills. The usual formula at the beginning of a will had normally been: 'I bequeath my soul to Almighty God, the Blessed Virgin Mary and all the holy company of heaven' This formula continues to be used until 1564, when for the first time, it becomes simply 'I bequeath my soul to Almighty God' By 1584 such phrases as 'my only redeemer' and 'faithfully believing that I shall attain to the joys prepared for the elect' are added, so it may be presumed either that Puritanism had taken hold, or that the then incumbent, who may well have written the wills at the direction of the legators, was of the reformist persuasion. In the majority of wills at all times, sums are left to St. Andrew's Church, though there is a change from 1558 onwards, the many bequests to various saints and altars being omitted. The last bequest to the High Altar is in 1558. Bequests to the mother church first of Lincoln and then to Peterborough, after the foundation of that diocese in 1541, also become rarer after the same date.

Priests could now marry, and the priest's house became a Rectory. Parish priests became less farmer-priests, living from tithes and their own farming efforts on glebe land, and much more country gentlemen, sons of local landowners, and graduates of one of the Universities. Terriers show that the church in 1633 still farmed 63 strips in the apparently five common fields, so lands continued to be tilled, and tithes paid.

Valentine Gregory, having purchased the advowson, now used his patronage almost as a family fief. In 1588 he appointed a relative, Thomas Gregory. At some unknown date before 1602, Thomas had got into trouble with the Consistory Court, where he was accused of 'committing fornication with his wife before marriage'. To compound this error, he had married outside the diocese of Peterborough in the city of Oxford. Nevertheless he was appointed Rector. Between 1592 and 1599 he had seven children. He died in 1602. Somewhat surprisingly, his wife outlived her husband. Next, in the same year, Valentine Gregory appointed Valentine Morley, another kinsman. In his will of 1611, William Gregory, who had inherited the advowson, left it to his eldest daughter, Joyce, with the proviso that, if she wished to sell it, she should sell it only to Valentine Morley or his son Theodore. Joyce married Richard Shortgrave, and the next rector in 1645 was William Shortgrave, who had been rector of Harpole in 1670. He married Grace, the daughter of Valentine Morley. He was succeeded in 1682 by his son William. By 1655, when the advowson was in the gift of Robert Shortgrave, the living which had been valued at £10 13s. 4d in 1291, was worth £96 per annum, a comfortable living at that time.

4 THE SIXTEENTH CENTURY VILLAGE

It was not only in the church that there were major changes. As profitable sheep farming developed in surrounding large estates even small farmers could add to their income with some sheep. The enclosures made by large landlords which gave rise to revolts and rebellions in other parts of the county would appear not to have affected this village. The common fields were not yet enclosed, and every family of any standing had a close round their dwelling, for the cultivation of the fruits and vegetables necessary for their own use, and the right to 'cow commons' i.e. to graze one or two animals on common land, seems to have been attached to most cottages. The heath, which supplied furze, peat and rough grazing was an additional resource, and parts were set aside for the poor in a section called appropriately Poors Heath.

This increasing prosperity is shown in the will of Richard Cart, made in 1600. This names him as a shepherd, which would seem to be a fairly lowly status, but from his legacies it is clear he was a prosperous man. He left more than £40 in monetary legacies and goods in an inventory totalling more than £96. His inventory also indicates that he had a parlour as well as a chamber, showing a good standard of comfort.

In the early years, only big landowners, like the de Brays, or the Lumleys, have left records. Parish registers start in 1570, though earlier records once existed but have not survived. Baptisms and marriages start in 1570, when eight baptisms and two marriages are recorded. Burials start in 1574, with eight funerals. There is a gap in baptismal records between 1708 and 1710, and in burials between 1614 and 1710. There is often a discrepancy between the recorded wills and the burial registers but these wills build up a picture of the community in the sixteenth and seventeenth centuries.

The earliest surviving will is of Ralph Messager in 1432. This is very like wills today, leaving bequests to his daughters and his sisters and other family members, and the residue to his wife. It is however written in latin, which was still the language of scholarship, the church and the law. Nicholas Jarman in 1499 simply leaves everything to his wife. By the sixteenth century wills are written in English, and have become more complex. Nearly seventy wills survive from that century in which legacies of sums of money are not uncommon, but the chief bequests are in land and property. Unfortunately there are few clues about the location of the properties bequeathed.

Such properties are generally left to the surviving spouse, or the eldest son. (The law at the time said that a widow was entitled to one-third of her husband's land on his death.) Ten of the surviving wills are from women, eight widows, and two apparently spinsters. Of these, Agnes Harris in 1546 very specifically leaves to 'Annes Harris daughter of Jone Harris' by special deed of gift, her house and land, and appoints Jone Harris as her sole executrix, keeping her whole estate in women's hands. An early feminist, perhaps?

An insight is given into the possessions which were most valued by bequests. Clothing is often specified; for example "to my father my best gown, ... to my brother in law a russet cote" (Thomas Stanton 1521). In 1545, Isabella Stanley leaves to her daughter 'my red kyrtell' (a gown). Household goods also figure frequently; bedlinens, such as blankets, pillows and sheets, pots and pans; pieces of furniture - 'coffers' 'cobbards' showing that these were prized articles. In a farming community animals are often mentioned – sheep, lambs, bullocks, and very occasionally horses.

In 1591 contributions to the Militia of corselets, calivers (a kind of fiearm) and muskets were required from Robert Andrew and Valentine Gregory. The militia was a band of men trained, though only with minimal training, to look after the defence of the county. The regular army served abroad. The constable made the list of men between the ages of 18 and 45, with exemptions made for Lords, ministers, men with three children, apprentices, articled clerks, the ailing or infirm. There were eleven other men liable for service or contributions, among them George Rigbie, John England, Richard England, John Storye and Valentine Lole. Many of these names were still found in the village in the twentieth century.

All in all, it seems that life in the village continued in traditional ways, moderately prosperous, largely independent from outside events, and virtually self-supporting. When trained bands were mustered in 1611, the Harleston levy was the highest in the three hundreds of Apelho, Wymersley, and Newbottle Grove at 28s 6d. In that trained band, five trained men are listed (Richard Harris, George Rigby, Richard Knight, Thomas Teacon, James Pilkgine) and 23 others. Names which appear in later centuries in the village history are Nelson, Travell, England, Smith, Fisher, Whiting, and Lack.

But major storms were brewing in the wider world.

The Civil War

Between 1642 and 1649, the conflict between King and Parliament came to a head and England was plunged into Civil War. Exactly where Harlestone stood in this conflict, and how it was affected, is a matter of putting together many small strands, rather than an exact record of history.

Northamptonshire as a county was fairly balanced in its attitudes, supporting

38

both sides almost impartially. Some of the big landowners, including the Spencers of Althorp, were naturally Royalists, but many others, like the Knightleys of Fawsley (to whom the Andrews were related) were Parliamentarians. The town of Northampton was solidly for Parliament. Harlestone, with no large landowners, gives few clues as to its allegiance but seems to have sided with Parliament. There is an anecdote that, during the 1930s, at a meeting where closer cooperation between the churches of St. Mary's, Brington and St. Andrew's, Harlestone was being discussed, it was said that the two could never work together because they had been on opposite sides during the Civil War! Since Brington, through the Spencers, was Royalist, this would put Harlestone on the side of Parliament. This would tie in with other evidence.

Although the war was principally over the issue of the divine right of the King, the religious element was strong. In broad terms, Anglicans were Royalists, and Parliamentarians Puritans. The rector of St. Andrew's throughout was Valentine Morley, appointed by Valentine Gregory, to whom he was related. He was succeeded in 1645 by William Shortgrave, who was married to Valentine Gregory's daughter, and their son William 'inherited' the living in 1682. This is the same family which bought the advowson from Henry VIII, and which had held on to it through all the storms of the Reformation. The Vicar of Bray comes strongly to mind! It should be noted that literacy was now more widespread. The Bible in English had been available since 1611, and the Book of Common Prayer, also in English, was in use in the churches. The proximity to Northampton, where many nonconformist sects flourished, and where there was strong support for Parliament, must also have influenced local attitudes.

On the other hand, Sir Lewis Dyve, a descendent of Henry de Bray who had now inherited Manor Farm, though living in Bedfordshire, was a strong royalist. He fought with distinction beside Prince Rupert in an encounter near Worcester in 1642. Since he was on the losing side, his estate in Harlestone was sequestered and sold by parliament in 1652. It was bought by a consortium of three gentlemen from Northampton and subsequently sold to the Andrew family, then building up an estate in Harlestone.

The war itself had impact only where lands were fought over, and plundered, or when young men were 'pressed' to serve in one or the other army. Harlestone was fortunate in that the main armies passed on either side, on the one hand up Watling Street towards Daventry, and on the other from Northampton towards Market Harborough on what is now the A508. The armies came close to the village on only two occasions: once in 1643 when a Royalist raiding party from Banbury made for Northampton via Daventry, Long Buckby, Holdenby and Chapel Brampton, missing Harlestone, and again in 1645 when the Parliamentarian Colonel Fairfax spent the night in Kislingbury and then brought his troops to Naseby, probably passing through Upper Harlestone, Great Brington, and on through East Haddon to the battlefield. Since they were on their way to action, there would have been no opportunity for serious looting and pillage. When an army passes it does not really matter whether it is friendly or unfriendly; the needs for plunder are the same. In other parts of the county there was much damage from both armies.

Harlestone did however figure in some events of the Civil War. When the King was imprisoned in Holdenby in 1645 he used to come to Althorp to play bowls, so must have been a familiar figure in the neighbourhood. In 1647 Cornet Joyce camped on Harlestone Heath on his way to fetch the King from Holdenby, to take him to London to his execution. It is reputed that during the Second Civil War, when the Scots army came as far south as Derby, militia from Northampton raised by the Earl of Halifax and Dr. Charles Doddridge, the famous dissident divine, assembled on the Heath to oppose the enemy. Perhaps fortunately the occasion never arose!

5 SEVENTEENTH CENTURY LIFE

That life continued through the turmoil of war is demonstrated by the races run from 1632 until 1739 on Harlestone Heath. The land was leased by William Lord Spencer (the second Baron Spencer) for £200. They were held on the Thursday of Easter Week yearly with cups given by local gentry. The races were later transferred to Northampton Racecourse, where they still have events called the Althorp Park stakes, and the Spencer Plate. Harlestone profited from these races. The Overseers of the Poor received annually sums of up to £1.50 for the relief of the poor of the parish.

One footnote; in 1727 the Spencer Plate, worth £16, was won by Sir Arthur Hesilrigg. His was the only horse in the race!

Throughout the century, law and order continued to be upheld in the traditional ways. Quarter sessions records tell not only of criminal offences, but also of civil matters. In 1631 Augustine Knight, husbandman, and William Cleaver, mason, were obliged to pay £10 and 20 shillings respectively in recognizances for refusing to 'goe and doe the same'. William Cleaver was fined 'for contempt of the constable'.

During the time of the Commonwealth (1649 –1660) religious conformity was strictly enforced. An account of offences is found in the Village Constables Bill of 1657, reported in the Quarter sessions records. It states that:

'We haue to acknowledge noe common cursers nor swearers, no open profaners of the Lord's Day, no recusants, noe buchers nor victulers that sell unholsome flesh nor malsters unholesome malt, noe houses of ill repute, noe ryots nor forceable entryes nor common quarrelers.'

On the other hand:

'our hue and cryes are duly executed, our watch and ward are duly kept, our waites and measures are sealed according to the standard, our highwayes are in good repair, our alehouse is lycensed and keep good order'.

It is difficult to believe that the village was so completely virtuous! The only real sinner seems to have been one William Davy, who was accused of 'keeping imperfect accounts and deteyning of towne money in his handes' He was also brought before the Quarter Sessions for 'breaking up the severall feild without consent of neighbores', so all in all he was a problem for the village.

In 1657 Ralph Rigbie of Harleston was bound over in the sum of £20 to keep

the peace "especially towards John Cox of Norton" Also in 1657 there was a riot in Harlestone led by several people from West Haddon and Long Buckby. They 'riotously and unlawfully assembled and gathered together to disturbe the publique peace and assaulted one Samuel Newman by force of arms so that his lyfe was dispared of'. This may well have had a religious dimension.

There are indications that there were dissenting families in the village. In the Hearth Tax Returns for 1674, Perseverence Whiting is listed. The name is an almost certain indication that she belonged to a family of puritans, though other Whitings are prominent as churchwardens in St. Andrew's Church. In Bishop Compton's census of 1695, nine nonconformists are listed for Harlestone, in contrast with none in Brington and three in Brampton. In addition, the only known emigrant from the village to the New World was Matthew Calmfield, a great-grandson of John Calmfield, who with his son, grandson and great-grandson is buried in the nave of the church. He went first to the Massachusetts Bay Colony, and later to Connecticut, where he became an important figure, being a Collector for Yale College, later Yale University, and one of the original patentees of the Charter of Connecticut. Many emigrants at that time went for religious reasons, so it is reasonable to suppose that he was a dissenter of some kind.

For minor offences, stocks were widely used until the nineteenth century; jail was generally reserved for offenders awaiting trial. Public humiliation was a major part of this punishment. The helpless victim would usually be mocked and abused, and pelted with anything which came to hand - rotten fruit and vegetables, mud, excrement, dead rats, even stones. The stocks in Harlestone were where there is now the garden of the Fox and Hounds. The village pound for straying animals was in the same area.

The village was by no means isolated, being only four miles from Northampton, where there was a market, and also on the main road from Northampton to Dunchurch.

John Ogilby's map

Speed's map of Northamptonshire in 1610 shows all the villages in the Newbottle Hundred, but no roads. In 1675, however, John Ogilby issued a landmark volume of maps of England and Wales. This is the first national road atlas of any country in Western Europe. In it the road from Northampton to Dunchurch is shown as diverging from today's A428 at Hopping Hill and crossing what is now New Duston to join Port Road, and continue through Upper Harlestone to pass Althorp, Brington and beyond. These early roads were little more than cart tracks. Road conditions generally were very bad, and were dealt with by piecemeal measures, until the Highway Act of 1553. By this, the duty of maintaining the roads fell on the parishes. Every parishioner had to provide 'one wain or cart furnished after the custom of the country and also two able men with the same' for four days each year, for every ploughland in tillage or pasture that he occupied, and so had every person keeping a horse or a plough in the parish. Every other householder, cottager or labourer had either to put in four days' labour or to send 'one sufficient labourer' in his stead. The four days were changed to six by Elizabethan legislation. Overseers or surveyors were appointed to carry out the necessary works. Unfortunately the records of the Overseers of the Highways in Harlestone have not survived.

In 1674, the Hearth Tax Returns show that there were 115 houses in Harlestone. Of these 95 had one hearth, and were therefore quite simple cottages, with fairly primitive living conditions. When dovecotes were no longer supplying sufficient saltpetre for the making of gunpowder, scrapings from peasants' cottage floors filled the gap! The more prosperous houses with two or three hearths would probably have been the larger farms. Of the larger houses, eleven had two hearths, five had three, the Rectory had six, and Thomas Andrew had twelve. One other resident, Thomas Stormer, had seven. This must have been either the vanished Bulmer House, or perhaps Grafton Lodge. Even in these early years there were some building regulations. In 1631 permission was granted for one John Blunt to build a house on land belonging to Robert Andrew since there was no suitable house otherwise available.

Inventories attached to wills are informative. The will of Elizabeth England in 1638, made on her deathbed by word of mouth is brief and to the point. : 'My goods I will shall go amongst my children and I make my brother Thomas Kirton executor.' These goods include seven pairs of sheets, ten napkins, two bedsteads, brass and pewter, 'company ware', and her wearing apparel. The witnesses were Robert Carr and William Kirton, and the inventory was valued in the sum of £26 14s. 10d by Thomas Gealing, William Kirton and Robert Carr. All these people appear in other documents of the time, and the mention in the wills helps to build up a picture of family relationships. In the same inventory, 'one Bible and other books' to a value of 8s. 8d. are listed, a rare example of literacy. These may have belonged to her husband who had died only a few months earlier. Sometimes there is clearly a story behind the legacy. Why, in 1666 did John Pettit leave sums of about £20 each to seven grandchildren, but to the eighth 'unto my grandchild Edward Whiting five shillings to buy him a pair of shoes'?

The wealthiest families in the seventeenth century (on the evidence of the wills) were the Andrews, the Gregorys, the Camfields and the Kertons, but many of the others left property and sums of money showing modest affluence. The Whiting and Stormer familes figure prominently. A lease dated 1562 for 'a messuage and lands in Harleston lately occupied by Edward Whitinge, deceased,' a close is named 'called the Wonge, close of pasture nigh the Lake Lane, holme of meadow called Whiting's Holme, and a yardland for 21 years." There were at that time two small lakes where there is now one. The Wonge was somewhere near the church, so this house is likely to have been Manor Farm. The Whitings were quarrymen as well as farmers. Their fine altar tombs in the churchyard are witness to their importance in the community. One is a rare example showing symbols of both stonemasons and freemasons on the same tomb.

Having bought the Lumley estate in 1500, and having now acquired Manor Farm, the Andrew family owned most of Harlestone. The village was no longer a small society of reasonably independent farmers, but a parish dependent on one major landowner, and one employer, the Andrews.

The Andrew Family

Thomas Andrew of Charwelton was descended from a very ancient family from Carlisle. After the Dissolution of the Monasteries in the sixteenth century, he had profited from the seizure of lands and had married Emma Knightley, daughter of Richard Knightley of Fawsley. His descendents from this marriage inherited and augmented their lands. By his second marriage to Elizabeth, daughter of Sir John Pulteney, he had a son, Richard, for whom he bought the Lumley Estate in Harlestone in 1499. During the next two centuries, the Andrews added to their estates in the parish, in 1652 the sequestered de Bray Estate, and later in 1753 most of the Bulmer Share.

By the end of the sixteenth century the descendents of Richard Andrew, who are almost alternately, and confusingly, called Thomas or Robert, lived in Harlestone. In an agreement made in 1582, the then Robert Andrew ordered a cartload of coals from Crick to be delivered to him in Harlestone, but it has not been possible to discover in which house he lived. Throughout this time they were adding to their estates more widely in the County, with properties in Creaton, Daventry, Drayton, Braunston, Staverton, and Northampton itself. The family was soon taking a prom-

44

inent part in local affairs. In the musters of Militia in 1586 and 1587, Thomas Andrew was to supply two demi-lances and 3 light horse (where Sir John Spencer was assessed at 3 demi-lances and 5 light horse). In 1591, 1595, and 1597, Robert Andrew was to supply armour - one corselet and one musket, and one demilance. In addition, in 1581 Edward Andrew, a cousin, who was rated at one light horse, appealed against this assessment, on the grounds that 'he was at law with Lord Cromwell and was impoverished, that his land was more chargeable than profitable and therefore prayed to be excused'. Whether he succeeded or not is not recorded.

Other related Andrews also occupied high positions. In 1567 a Sir Thomas Andrew was High Sheriff of Northamptonshire, and was present at the execution of Mary Queen of Scots in Fotheringhay Castle. Interestingly, when in 1799 Robert Andrew of Harlestone married Frances Packe of Prestwold, Leicestershire, a cross which was reputed to have belonged to the ill-fated Queen passed to her. This has now been shown to have formed part of a rosary, very tiny but beautifully carved, with the Resurrection on one side and the Assumption of the Virgin on the other. It passed down through the Packe family and is now in the National Museum of Scotland. It is almost certainly the relic which was given to Sir Thomas Andrew in 1567, as it has been authenticated as being from the right period.

The Robert Andrew who died in 1604 bequeathed … 'my bodie being made of earth I bequeath in to the earth againe to be buried in the North Ile of the parish church of Harleston aforesaid neare the place there where Elizabeth my late well beloved wife lieth buried'. There is no trace of a memorial in that position. All the Andrew memorial plaques are on the south wall. There is, however, a family vault underneath the North Aisle of the church, long since closed up, but the entrance to which can be traced outside the church.

In 1650, Thomas Andrew, the then owner of the estate, died in Harlestone. He left an inventory to a value of £792 2s, 2d. The house he occupied was a

Robert Andrew died 1829

farmhouse, with stables, dairies, barns and yards, a mixed farm, where he had arable crops of wheat and rye. milk cows, bullocks and a bull, pigs and poultry, and nearly one thousand sheep. The house was comfortable, with a hall, which was clearly a reception room with a fireplace, chairs and tables, a Little Parlour, an Upper Parlour, (each carpeted with tables, chairs and cupboards,) a master bedroom, with adjoining closet containing a desk, and shelves – so a sort of study – and in addition a brushing chamber, containing wardrobes and chests, and his clothes. There was an upper chamber, and a middle chamber, and a schoolroom – this for seven children! – and a servant's room with three beds In the Store Chamber was the household linen; two pairs of linen sheets, 16 pairs of coarser hempen sheets, and 4 pairs of harden (a coarse cloth). ten pairs of pillow cases, six towels, twelve table cloths and twelve dozen napkins. The kitchen quarters were the kitchen itself, a dry larder, a wet larder and a buttery. He had a dairy, a bakehouse and a brewhouse. Interestingly no silver or brass items are recorded, though they must have existed, and are frequently inventoried. This property was beside a meadow called 'the homes' which was left to a younger son. If this meadow is identified as the 'Home Close' recorded in the sale map of 1832, (which is problematic) it would place this Andrew farm in Lower Harlestone.

In 1650 Richard Andrew, uncle to Thomas, was a Justice of the Peace, and in 1668 and 1676 Thomas himself was High Sheriff. During the Civil War, Robert Andrew of Harlestone, his son, appears to have supported the Commonwealth, receiving a letter of thanks from Oliver Cromwell in 1655 when he gave up the post of High Sheriff, but his name appears again among the persons taking oaths of allegiance in 1673, after the return of the Stuart Dynasty. His son Robert was

High Sheriff in 1669, and his nephew and heir carried on the family tradition by being High Sheriff in 1688 and 1689, and M.P. for Higham Ferrars in 1690 and for Northampton in 1701. The family rode the political and religious storms of the time with success, and retained their lands throughout.

As a family, they seem to have been addicted to country pursuits – hunting, shooting fishing, horse breeding – but also to have had a quarrelsome streak. In several generations, anecdotes surface about their bad relations with their neighbours. When an eighteenth century Andrew was out hunting. His hounds strayed on to Spencer land, and the gamekeeper shot one of them. Shortly afterwards, he met Lord Spencer out riding, and apparently trespassing on Andrew land, so he shot his horse! Curiously, it appears that the two gentlemen were later very friendly. A later Robert Andrew even had an altercation with a stag. When he wounded the animal while out hunting in Harlestone park, it ran at him and tossed him. The incident is recorded in an amusing conversation Piece painting by the artist James Millar, which is now in the possession of Northamptonshire Record Society, and hanging on loan in the Judges' Lodgings in Northampton.

6   THE EIGHTEENTH CENTURY

The century started with a storm, an appropriate beginning for a century of many changes. The rector, the Revd Shortgrave, wrote that 'on a Sunday in 1702 there was a hurricane at Harleston that passed on, as it were, in a glade of a hundred yards in breadth. Within this space it swept off huge branches of trees, twisted a maple like a faggot band, swept off almost every tree in John Mannings' orchard in Harleston, stript some houses and committed other outrages. It reached from Harleston to Northampton. In Sepulcre's church they observed it just expiring'.

Parish registers are now much more complete. From 1719 – 1760, of the 173 people whose occupations were mentioned in the baptismal register, thirtytwo different occupations are recorded. 46 men were employed in the quarries, 46 were labourers, and 34 were farmers in some way. In the retail trades, only 3 (butcher, victualler, shopkeeper) appear.

All the others are practical specialities, such as carpenters and shoemakers, and another 11 were involved with sheep as shepherds, woolcombers and weavers. Farming remained the main occupation, subject to the ususal problems of agricultural life. It was hit in 1746 by a severe outbreak of cattle distemper, which decimated cattle herds. Infected beasts were destroyed and their hides cut to pieces. Farmers were compensated but only to half the value of the animals. The churchwardens paid 4 shillings for a book recording the proclamation of this disease and also the 'cessation of distemper of the cows'.

The Lumley name continued in the parish. In 1721 a Thomas Lumley did homage at Court, and in 1767 Tubalcain Lumley the elder and younger were named as having allotments which paid towards the Poor Law administration, the elder for £9 18s. 5d and the younger for £4 18s. 4d., quite considerable sums at the time. A Thomas Lumley was also named as having two houses and a little close which still paid tithes.

The family therefore was well represented in the village, and from 1710 onwards several held office as Overseers of the Poor, Constables, Overseers of the Highway and Churchwardens.

In 1743 Thomas Lumley the Elder, stonecutter, left to his wife Dorothy "the mesuage which was formerly a barn and lately converted into a dwelling house and now in the occupation of my eldest son Thomas Lumley." It would seem that the Lumleys continued to live there intermittently for the next 100 or so years. This is possibly the present Dovecote House.

Being now the largest landowners in the parish, the Andrews decided to build themselves a suitable house. In 1715 they built the first Harlestone House, known as Harlestone Park.

Harlestone Park

It was a rectangular building, with the main entrance from Church Lane, beside the school. The house now on the right of the pillared entrance is the original Lodge. The pillared gateposts are the original eighteenth century ones, and are Grade II listed. There was in the valley of the brook a string of two or more small ponds. A dam was built over the brook, thus creating an ornamental lake where previously there had been two small lakes.

Notice the simple path over the dam, and the entrance on the north side of the brook, compared with the present day.

Harlestone House is reputed to have been the model for Mansfield Park in Jane Austen's novel of that name, though Cottesbrooke House also claims that distinction. Two letters which might settle the matter, from Jane Austen to a Miss Martha Lloyd while staying with the Andrews, should be in Northampton Record Office, but they have unaccountably vanished. What is certain is that the 1820 edition of the book has Harlestone House as a frontispiece and that, among other topographical features mentioned, Mansfield Heath where the party in the story go riding, strongly resembles Harlestone Heath, and the 'pleasant ride' over the Pond bridge through the new pheasantry and along the turnpike vividly recalls the environs of Harlestone House.

When the house was eventually sold in 1940 to demolition contractors and pulled down, in the roof was found a carved board which read "Benjamin Noon of Dafentrey and Richard England of Harleston Hed Carpenters built this hous and all the buildings and layed all the floores. Cuie mode sue sorte contentues". It was dated 1728, presumably when the house was completed. The name of England appears regularly in village records, and they are very often carpenters. In the 1950s, Arthur England, one of their descendents, built the organ still being used in the church. He was also the village undertaker.

A New Road System

The only drawback to their fine new home as far as the Andrews were concerned was that the traditional route connecting all parts of the village passed right by their back door. So, as people could in those days, they simply closed the road! This broke the link and effectively split the village into two parts. In Eyre's map of 1789, the road through the village down Church Lane is still clearly running through the estate marked 'Robt. Andrew Esq.' It is probable that this is an error, and that the route was surveyed at an earlier date, since the map was revised in 1779 and again in 1791.

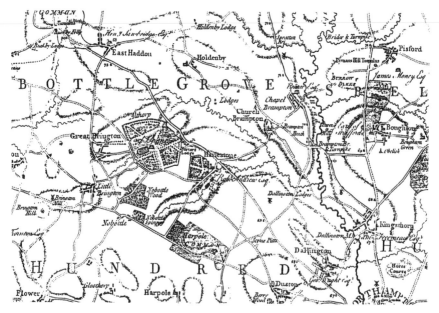

In 1738 came the first turnpike. This road is now the A428. It was a stretch between Northampton and Dunchurch, and part of the extensive network which over very few years transformed communications in England. With better surfaces travel time was cut, and post coaches provided a reliable public transport network. Mail could be delivered from London to any part of England in two days. The new road bypassed the village, and crossed the brook first by a ford, and then on a small bridge. When the curbs were put down the sides of the road in September 1936, the old brick bridge was demolished and a concrete one on iron bars constructed. As the old bridge was being removed, it was possible to see that a roadway had originally run through the stream, immediately under the present bridge.

Virtually all the houses along this stretch of road in Lower Harlestone date from the time of the turnpike, One cottage has on the gable the initials LJM 1774. The Old House has a sundial which says 'Watch and Pray' and 'The hour is at hand'. When a cottage at the foot of the hill was being restored in the early 1990s, walled into the chimney was a woman's shoe. Shoes which hold the shape of the wearer more than any other garment, were often built into chimneys to bring good luck. This particular shoe dated from c 1750 and is an example of typical everyday wear in the mid-eighteenth century. Notable is the Fox and Hounds Inn, a fine eighteenth century house, which catered principally for passing traffic. It is mentioned in the Enclosure Act of 1767, when the licensee was Alice Stamp. It was in the 1730s the meeting place of Trustees for the Turnpike in the area and is also mentioned in the Turnpike Trust Minute Book. The smithy next door still recalls the need for farrier's help on such roads. Smiths were then as ubiquitous as small garages in the early days of motoring.

Towards the end of the century the New Road was built, looping round the Park of Harlestone House, to join the Northampton road at the top of the hill. In the Enclosure document of 1779, this road is mentioned, among others which again define boundaries. This road system is essentially the one which endures to the present day. It is the reason why it is so difficult to get from the church, for example, to Upper Harlestone, and why Lower Harlestone developed almost as a separate entity.

John Clendon's Tithe Book

In 1710 John Clendon replaced William Shortgrave as the new Rector of Harlestone. The house he lived in was handsome but fairly modest.

At the beginning of the century he had a problem. 'The hearth of ye chimney in ye chamber over ye cellar will not bear a great fire to be made on it for under the stone there is a piece of timber (it seems) which will be like to catch & endanger ye house, if the said hearth stone be set with fire that is for this reason I have put up some iron bars & not made fire upon ye hearth.' The windows on the ground floor were closed up, not to escape window tax, but in order to prevent coachmen looking in when on their high coaches.

He took a great interest in the garden. He has left a list of the flowers he grew, especially auriculas and carnations. The varieties of both appear to be largely unknown today. For auriculas (a variety of primula) he lists such varieties as Picatee, King of Bohemia, the elephant, and the nymph, and for carnations, Ravishing Flame, the Bedford Tory, and the Queen of Sheba. He also had a vegetable garden. In 1741 he engaged a gardener named Tom Pain at a rate of eight pence a day.

He found that during the long tenure of the Gregory/Shortgrave clan, no records had been kept of the tithes which should have been paid. He made a note to ask Mrs. Shorgtgrave, William's widow, whether an Easter book was kept and what was demanded for the Easter Offering (traditionally the 'perk' of the rector). Then he wanted details of the tithes : "Whither any tithe calves, whither any tythe Pidgeons, whither the tythe of brakes in Broom close and other places, whither herbage of becks and othr lands, whither tythes Honey & wax, whither tythes of ye mill." This also illustrates the very wide scope of the tithes demanded amounting to a tenth of the produce of the parish.

For the next fifty years, he kept careful track of what was due to him. This involved frequent disputes with his parishioners. Tithes, like any tax, were much resented and farmers went to great lengths to avoid them. In notes he kept at the back of his account books, John Clendon vents his anger at these tricks – not milking cows 'clean' when his share was due, selling lambs just before tithe day, and constant minor wars about grazing rights and the like.

With Robert Andrew he was on very bad terms. "He woud always lend an ear against me, to even ye vilest & most scandalous of ye Town, right or wrong; & not hear me when I mentiond any to him in my vindication; saying I came not to visit him but about business." He complained that he would "Horse-race upon ye Poors Brakes & not make amends: Take ye Poors Furze away in ye Hays by Brampton; Remove ye pound against ye parsons wall & horned cattell break it down; Rabbits over-run ye common; Foxes kept yt destroy ye neighbours poultry; Diggs pool in Deepdale on ye common; Enclose pt of ye comon on ye top of y allys & plant trees on't". The litany of complaints is endless. He could do nothing right. Robert Andrew was '… Angry when I dont visit him, & yet uses me ill wn I do….'

Another complaint related to the closing of the road. 'Stops ye church way throu ye wong now calld ye Park' At the same time he moved a cross. 'Cross by ye new house taken away & ye ground taken up by ye house' This cross is quite probably the one which stood in Upper Harlestone where the chestnut tree now stands, and

Harlestone Church and Rectory in the early nineteenth century, by George Clark of Scaldwell

which was reputed to be a preaching cross. Only shards now remain, making it impossible to prove one way or another.

A more serious accusation was interference with Harlestone charities. "There is about 11 pounds given yearly to ye Poor of this Parish at St. Thomas, from lands lying in Nether Shuckborough in Warwickshire, which usd to be distributed by ye minister of Harleston & ye officers of ye parish; & which for some years I had a hand in ye distribution of, as had my predecessor; But finding that what was orderd by us ye minister & officers of ye said parish to ye poor respectively was altered & otherwise disposed of by Mr. Andrews order & since solely by Mr. West his butler, I have for some time refused to have any concern in ye affair" Since this charity financed the school, it was a major interference with custom.

Harlestone School

From its foundation c. 1710 the school was supported by these Harlestone Charities, an organisation set up c. 1708 with £200 left to 'the poor of Harlestone'. In 1739, Henry Lovell added to the funds with a gift of £50. Properties were purchased in Kislingbury and in Shuckburgh, Warwickshire, and the income used partly for the relief of poverty, and partly to support a school. Except when Robert

Andrew interfered, it was administered by the Rector and the churchwardens. The school continued to be financed in this way until it became a National School in 1811.

The first recorded schoolmaster in was Richard Gealing in 1715. He is mentioned in Morton's Natural History of Northampton:

"To pass on now to remarkable imperfections in the body of man. One instance of this we find in the limbs of a young man Richard Gealing of Halston. His hand and wrist from the ulna and radius are turned outwards. Both right hand and left hand in like manner. His hamstrings are contracted and his legs grown across each other. The imperfection is strange, yet not as wonderful as is the lad's ingenuity and industry in relieving himself under this misfortune. He has learned to write, and to cast accounts, with so much exactness that he is now himself the master of a school, wherein he teaches those arts to admiration and which is still more considerable, as the position of his hands is such that he is forced to look behind him when he writes, and by reason of the disorderly structure of his fingers, he can hold his pen in no other way than betwixt the three middle fingers outward, and the little finger and thumb within, which are the bearers of the pen; yet he flourishes and draws too with his pen with a skill and dexterity beyond what anyone could imagine or expect of such a miserable lame man."

This would seem to be the same Richard Gealing who features in the accounts of the Overseers of the Poor from 1711 onwards for sums generally of 2 shillings per week, with additional sums for lodging, clothes washing and carrying 'turves and bushes' for fuel, and significantly for making and repairing his shoes. It would seem that the Overseers also paid for his training as a teacher. In 1716, 16 shillings is paid for 'the cirtificate for Richard Gealing'. In 1721 he died.

The school in which he taught was not the present building. The premises then were three cottages on the South side of Cooch's Lane, where the school stayed until the nineteenth century. The lower cottage was the schoolmasters house, (an arched door distinguishes it), and the middle one the infants' school. That a school was necessary is shown by the illiteracy rates which between 1754 and 1812 are recorded as 39% of males, and 61% of females.

Enclosures

During this century the change to permanent enclosure of land accelerated, especially as parts of the fields were amalgamated into larger areas. This movement is illustrated by the number of names found in the documents relating to strips in fields. In 1710 twenty seven names appear. By 1761, this number has shrunk

Park Farm House in the twentieth century

to eight, the eight being Andrew, Lumley, Manning, Jackson, Whiting, Starmer, Callis, and Cooch. In 1766, Harlestone was enclosed by Act of Parliament, and the system of strip farming came to an end. The chief gainer from the Act was Robert Andrew, Lord of the Manor. Also named are, among others, Earl Spencer, Thomas Cooch, Benjamin West, Simon Callis, and two cottagers, Thomas Kerton and Joseph Gross.

The Rector at the time was Gilbert Andrew, the brother of Robert Andrew, and between them they made an arrangement which allowed Robert Andrew to use the lands behind the rectory which had traditionally been Glebe lands. The church got the lands on the far side of the A428, where Glebe Farm is now situated. A new rectory was built in Upper Harlestone, now called Park Farm House, with reference to the old glebe farm, and this remained the rectory until 1845.

New farms were now placed in the centre of singly owned fields. Any farm in the middle of fields – Fleetland Farm, Glebe Farm, Mill Farm – is a post-enclosure farm.

There is no map of the Harlestone enclosures, but very detailed descriptions are given of the extent of the allotments to the major beneficiaries. Boundaries are still easily recognizable, such as Brampton Brook, Harlestone Brook, the Turnpike (the A428), and the Brampton Road. Rights on the heath are specified, including the cutting of turves, showing that peat was still a common fuel. All hedges, ditches and fences on these properties are to be maintained at the expense of the new owners. There is plainly some concern for equity between larger landowners and allocation of the new rights, but small holders lost out badly.

For better or worse, enclosures have created the landscape we have today. It is curious that the hedgerows, which we now struggle to preserve as part of our heritage, only date, for the most part, from the mid-eighteenth century.

Under the earlier system, even someone who had only one strip could feed his family by using his rights on the common fields for grazing, and the heath for fuel. The new system may have been more efficient, and brought in more income for larger landowners, but it created a new landscape and a new class of agricultural poor. The Northamptonshire poet, John Clare, born in Helpston, near Peterborough, (which was then in Northamptonshire), was the son of poor farming labourers, and took a highly critical view of the change:

Then came enclosre – ruin was her guide
But freedoms clapping hands enjoyed the sight
Tho comforts cottage soon was thrust aside
And workhouse prisons raised upon the scite....

Poor relief now came into prominence. Until the Dissolution of the Monasteries, poor relief had been in the hands of the Church. After the Reformation it was not until 1601 that an Act was passed placing the relief of poverty in the hands of the parishes. It was financed by a levy on all yardlands, and the income gradually rose during the early years of the century, from around £20 in 1710, until in 1757 it amounted to £159. Two Overseers of the Poor were appointed each year, and their accounts were monitored by the Rector, and by two outside referees. The sums dispensed were small – a few pence to an average of ten people, frequently widows or for care in sickness. In 1708, 6d was paid for half a pint of white wine for John Stacey – apparently an invalid because other sums are paid for his care. The sums for nursing care tend to end with the costs of burial: bell, grave and affidavit costing about one shilling. The affidavit was to certify that the body had been buried in a woollen shroud, which was required by law to help domestic wool producers. By 1766 there are twenty recipients, and many more payments for more general purposes, for example to a doctor for regular attendances. There seems to have been a fair amount of humanity in these payments. The young man, very crippled, who later became a schoolmaster in Harlestone, was greatly helped by the Overseers.

As enclosures took hold, there was a sharp increase in the number of claimants. The parish registers also show this increase. In 1784 for the first time the word 'pauper' appears instead of the usual trade or profession of the deceased. In 1786, of the eleven deaths in the register four are given as paupers, including names such as Dent, Lack and Line which in the past had been associated with families of some standing in the parish. Poor families were boarded out, generally with widows, who had earlier been receiving benefits, but who were now paid for their care of others, and there were two parish cottages behind Rock Farm, which later became extremely dilapidated and were demolished. Some cottages were later re-formed into a workhouse. In November 1746 there was an advertisement in the Northampton Mercury for "any proper person willing to undertake the care of a workhouse... to contact the Churchwardens and Overseers" This first workhouse was used only for the reception of poor inhabitants who needed help, and was divided by partitions.

Towards the end of the eighteenth century there were 101 families in Harlestone. In 107 houses two families lived, and 4 or 5 houses were uninhabited. The exodus from the land following on industrialisation was already under way.

Enclosures changed the pattern of employment in Harlestone. Many more men were named in the registers simply as labourers, working on other men's farms and in the quarries. The great house which the Andrews had built, called at that time Harlestone Park, also employed many men, and provided alternative employment for women which may well have been not unwelcome, since, however restrictive, it was probably easier than agricultural work in all weathers. There was even a healer of sorts, called Richard Cross, who advertised in 1766 in the Northampton Mercury: ' Notice is hereby given that Richard Cross of Harlestone infallibly cures ruptures, etc in either sex from one year old to sixty. Has made a perfect cure of Thomas Harris, son of Samuel Harris, Baker, of the town of Northampton, after being rendered incurable by several eminent physicians'.

Voting patterns show the shrinking number of independent farmers at this time. Voting was not as it is today. It was very public. Certain property qualifications were necessary to have a vote at all, and the names of the voters and where they placed their votes were recorded openly in a book all might read. The lengths candidates went to to ensure victory are legend. Drinks were certainly lavishly given.

In Harlestone there were in 1702 and 1705 31 voters, who all voted the Whig interest, probably largely because Lord Spencer was one of the candidates. Again in 1705 the same voters voted for Whig candidates. (Broadly, Tories were for the King and tradition, and Whigs for Parliament and reform). In 1730 on the death of Sir Justinian Isham the local gentlemen and clergy put up his son as their candidate without informing the freeholders, who promptly put up their own candidate, William Hanbury, and voted him in. There were by now only 15 voters with the necessary property qualification. In 1748 the Harlestone voters elected William Knightly and William Hanbury but by then there were only 7 voters, and by 1806 the number had shrunk to four.

Crime continued to be severely punished, the death penalty being common for theft but most reported crimes in the village seem to have been minor ones. On March 25, 1765 a notice appeared in the Northampton Mercury: "Stolen from James Southam of Harleston about the latter end of June last a HIVE OF BEES and on Saturday, 16th of this month another hive of bees was stolen from the same place. Whoever will give intelligence of the said bees, so as they may be had again, shall receive half a Guinea reward of me James Southem" Whether he found the culprit is not recorded. The Constables Accounts of Expenditure between 1729 and 1832 have many entries for disabled soldiers and sailors passing through the village – a consequence of the Continental wars in which England was involved – and also for duties at the Assizes and general peacekeeping, for the suppression of vermin, and the maintenance of the pound and stocks.

A more serious crime took place in 1792, and was very fully recorded in the Northampton Mercury. The general tone of the report makes a strong contrast with crime reporting today, and is worth quoting in full.

"Yesterday James Cross and Thomas Smith were executed here pursuant to their sentence at our fall assizes, for robbing and cruelly beating Richard Manning of Great Brington. Cross was a native of Harlestone, and Smith of Long Buckby, both in this county. The behaviour of these unhappy men after their trial was very penitent and becoming. On the day before their execution they confessed to a number of robberies in which themselves and their accomplices had been concerned: by which it appears that Smith though a young man, but 21, had been an old offender. Cross, who was about the same age, did not commence his career of public depredations till November last, when, having been drinking freely at a public house, on his way home he met with Smith, by whom he was easily persuaded to become his accomplice in stealing a goose from Mr. Hanwell, of Buckby; - from one step they proceeded to another, till the perpetration of the crime for which they suffered, which was the seventh robbery they had committed together. There is an amiable trait in the human heart, that when a fellow creature comes to pay down his life as a forfeiture for his crimes, we are apt to forget his offences, however enormous, and to view him with an eye of sympathy; in short, resentment is superseded by pity; so was it in this instance, the feelings of the multitude appearing to be interested in a high degree. ... At the place of execution their exhortations to the populace were uncommonly fervid - earnestly entreating them to avoid drunkenness and Sabbath-breaking to which they attributed their ruin, - an admonition they frequently repeated; and after some time spent in prayer, in which their invocations to heaven were particularly audible and fervent, they were launched into eternity. Thus perished the mortal parts of men, who but for the fatal bias of inordinate

The tablet to Sir Salathiel Lovell by Edward Stanton in St Andrew's Church, Harlestone

passions and depraved habits, might have added to the general flock of usefulness in society, and have been a comfort to their connections. May the recollection of their untimely exit prove a friendly beacon to the Sabbath-breaker and the drunkard, and warn them to avoid those fatal rocks upon which their bark was wreck'd!"

Sir Salathiel Lovell

In 1709 Sir Salathiel Lovell bought an estate in Harlestone from the Dyve family. This is apparently the residue of the ancient Bulmer estate, since it carried with it the right of the owner to call himself Lord of the Manor of Harlestone. The use of this title greatly annoyed the Andrew family and at the first opportunity they had the house demolished. According to Bridges, "the house was taken down a few years since by the present Mr. Andrew". The site of this house remains a mystery. Of the known house platforms, all are too small to mark the residence of so important a family, but without an expert archaeological survey no firm conclusion can be drawn.

Sir Salathiel was born in 1632, and died at the age of eighty one in 1713. He was a lawyer, at one time Recorder of London, and latterly recorder of Northampton. In his Autobiography, Richard Lovell Edgeworth wrote: "In 1732 my father married Rachel Jane Lovell, daughter of Samuel Lovell, a Welsh judge, who was the son of Sir Salathiel Lovell, that Recorder of London who, at the trial of the seven bishops in the reign of James II proved himself to be a good man though he was but an indifferent lawyer." This trial led to the Glorious Revolution of 1688. The seven bishops had refused to read the King's Declaration of Indulgence, suspending the laws against Roman Catholics and Dissenters and admitting them to civil and military posts, which the King sent to be read from all parish pulpits. They were acquitted by a jury on 30th June, 1688 and that night an invitation was sent to William of Orange to become King. Harlestone was thus doubly represented. One of the seven Lords who formed the delegation was the Earl of Scarborough, who traced his ancestry back to Harlestone through the Lumley line.

So Sir Salathiel came to Harlestone with a reputation and a great career behind him. As recorder of Northampton he was involved in the rebuilding of Northampton after the Great Fire of 1675. He had a son, Henry and a daughter, Maria. Henry died in 1724 at the age of 48, so enjoyed his inheritance for a very short time. In the Court Roll of Harlestone of 1721 is recorded Baron Henry Lovell of the Manor House in Harlestone. His sister Mary had married Joseph Townsend of London, and her son Samuel, who had adopted the Lovell name – presumably when he inherited in 1724 – is buried in the same tomb as his mother in Harlestone church. Henry's daughter Mary married Viscount Barrington, who sold the Manor

Harlestone House c 1820

of Harlestone in 1753 for £5152. 19s. to three people, one of whom was John Andrew of Creaton, the father of Robert Andrew of Harlestone. The inheritance still included many farms, and rents from stone pits, which provided an income for the family even in 1751 and 1752.

The Lovells were in Harlestone for a very short time, yet their memorials in the church are the most impressive. The fine tablet to Sir Salathiel by Edward Stanton is in a baroque style, and two others, also probably by Stanton, are for Lady Lovell (1718) and for Maria Townsend in 1743.

Harlestone House

By the end of the eighteenth century, Harlestone Park did not please the then Robert Andrew, and in 1809 he commissioned the Repton Brothers to modernise and redesign the property, from then on called Harlestone House.

This decision seems extraordinary in view of his circumstances at that time. In April, 1799, his mother had died in a dreadful accident at Harlestone Park. Her clothes caught fire and she was so badly burned that she died the next day. One month later, Robert married Frances Packe, daughter of James Packe of Leicestershire. She died in childbirth in October, 1800, and as the memorial plaque in the church states "Her infant son did not survive his mother". Yet, bereft of a direct heir, widowed and alone, - he never remarried - in 1809 he commissioned the re-design of his house. To add to the mystery, he was also in financial straits. Robert was a heavy gambler, and addicted to horseracing. He was also a bad manager, not having rents collected, and selling off family properties in other parts of the county to meet his most pressing debts. Yet the new house was much larger and more impressive than the earlier one.

A new entrance was made from the corner of the A428 and the New Road, with a rustic 'cottage orné' as the entrance lodge. An impressive Orangery was added on the west side. The new driveway swept across the park, to cross like a pretty seven arched bridge over the small dam which had created the ornamental lake. On the lake was a boathouse. The grounds were landscaped by the Reptons.

Humphrey Repton, in his Notebooks, tells an anecdote about his experiences in doing this. He found a number of great elms among the oaks in the park, which he wished to remove because they were overshadowing the oaks, but he did not dare to suggest so radical a solution. In November, 1810, however, there was a great storm which uprooted all the elms, and left standing all but one of the oaks '…producing exactly the effect of improvement which I had anticipated but had not dared to recommend…' The occurrence was recorded on a tablet inscribed 'Genio loci' (to the spirit of the place).

The house was built of Harlestone stone, but was plastered and painted white, and was known locally as the White House. The Reptons brought the entrance round to the north front, and added a west wing, to match the already existing east wing, giving a new and elegant drawing room. New kitchens were added and stables and a coach house also built to the east of the main house. There were 15 bedrooms, many with dressing rooms adjoining, but only one bathroom. Baths were still normally brought to the rooms of the residents.

Robert Andrew enjoyed his new home until 1829, when he died, but by then he was already negotiating to sell the property in order to meet his debts, which were very large, through his addictions to gambling and horse racing and breeding. The walled paddocks, now playing fields are a relic of his horse breeding activities. After his death, his brother-in-law, Colonel Packe, managed to sell the estate to the Spencers of Althorp in 1832, and from that time on virtually the whole of Harlestone has remained in the hands of the Spencer family.

The Spencers

From the time they first bought the Althorp estate in 1508 the Spencers, as neighbours, appear from time to time in the history of Harlestone. But it was only in

1832, when the fourth Earl Spencer bought Harlestone Park from the heirs of Robert Andrew that a close association began. The estate included Harlestone House, the Fox and Hounds public house, the Rectory, several farms, a large number of cottages, and a family pew with a fireplace in St. Andrew's Church.

The fourth Earl was a generally benevolent landlord. In 1851 he took all the employees on the estate to the Great Exhibition in the Crystal Palace, with all expenses paid, substantial refreshments in Hyde Park, and nothing deducted from their wages. Housing for employees was also well above the standard usually associated with tied properties. In 1851, for estate workers' housing, he appointed the architect Edward Blore, who also designed Buckingham Palace, the Vorontsov Palace in the Ukraine, and estate cottages for other members of the nobility. These are the the the Ten Cottages on the A428. The datestone shows 1851, with the Spencer Arms. They formed a planned layout with accompanying washhouses. The same model can be seen in many neighbouring villages on the Spencer Estate. They were in their day model dwellings, and are still very desirable in modern times and are today Grade II listed.

The fifth earl, who inherited the title in 1857, continued in the same vein. He had a distinguished political career, twice being Viceroy of Ireland, but in spite of his high position in the establishment, his political ideas were very liberal with a small 'L'. He made acute comments on the situation in the United States during a visit there just before the War between the States began, strongly opposing slavery, but understanding the complicity of mill–owners in this country who relied on American cotton, produced by slave labour. During his time as Viceroy in Ireland, he tried to introduce a fairer system of landlord-tenant relationships, but Gladstone refused his proposals. In a wish to promote fairer systems generally, he put his philosophical ideas into practice in his activities in Harlestone. This took the form of encouraging co-operatives. In 1887 he set up a cooperative farm of 800 acres with eight co-operators and a manager. Lord Spencer provided the working capital, and net profits were carried to a reserve for repayment of the original capital. A quarter of the profits were to be set aside, to be divided according to the proportion of wages earned by the co-operators during the year. Unfortunately it was a time of agricultural depression, and through a combination of this, bad prices for farm produce, and quarrelling among the co-operators about their shares, the experiment was a failure. The loss of the first balance sheet was £207. 9s. 7d. and on the second £672 1s. 5d. Some of the loss was a paper loss, but nevertheless the actual financial loss carried by Lord Spencer was £80. His friend Lord Suffolk, who took an interest in this experiment, wrote to him:

"I sincerely hope that you may reap the reward you deserve for your kindness and

enterprise. At the same time, as kicks rather than half pence are the usual guerdon of philanthropists, you will probably meet the result, whatever it may be, with philosophic composure."

He also helped in 1862 in setting up a co-operative village store in Lower Harlestone which had varying success. It became the Cooperative Society which did business at the Fox and Hounds in 1886 and later at the Post Office, an outdoor beer licence being attached. A new branch grocery was opened adjoining the Fox and Hounds in 1887. In 1898 John Warren became Manager of Harlestone Industrial Society Ltd., grocers, drapers and beer retailers. In 1903 George Dunkley was manager, but from 1910 onwards no managers are listed by name. The business continued apparently to flourish until 1940, when the name changes to Harpole Industrial and Provident Society. There was also a Cooperative Dairy Association set up in 1890, using the old Maulting premises for place of business. This too foundered when agricultural depression made it unviable.

Another project to the benefit of the village which was undertaken in the time of this Earl, was the provision of a sewage plant. This was a reed bed filtration plant, situated in the lower reaches of the brook, near its junction with Brampton Brook. Together with the ingenious system of piping water from Yew Tree farm to cottages in Upper Harlestone, this ensured that in that part of the village at least, services were for the period very good.

Harlestone House was occupied by various members of the Spencer family. It was Captain the Honorable Frederick Spencer, who, during his tenancy, presented to St. Andrew's Church in 1845 the lectern copy of the Bible which was used until it was superseded by a modern translation of the Scriptures. Frederick was a keen member of the Jockey Club, and owned a champion horse called Cotherstone, which was the founder of the Althorp stud. On the wall of one of the paddocks in the Playing Field enclosure is a plaque, now almost illegible, commemorating this horse, and recording his ancestry '… foaled by Touchstone… won the 2000 guineas at Newmarket and the Derby stakes at Epsom…'

From 1877 to 78 while, Althorp was being remodelled, the sixth Earl Spencer lived there. He was a very strict parent, and his young family was much happier at Harlestone where they had fewer duties and supervision was not so strict as at Althorp. In her old age, Sarah Spencer wrote of the stay in Harlestone House and the eventual return to Althorp '….it was a happy affectionate time to all, and the removal from Harlestone was a grief in itself…' The last tenant from 1891 onwards was the Duchess of Grafton, who remained there until her death in 1928.

7 THE NINETEENTH CENTURY VILLAGE

The Spencers were the major landowner, and nearly everyone worked for them either in agriculture or in the two great houses, Althorp and Harlestone House, living in tied cottages on the Estate.

The repeal of the corn laws which had such beneficial effects for the price of bread for the manufacturing cities, had the opposite effect on home grown grains which could not compete with the mass production from the vast prairies of North America. The forties were known as 'the hungry forties' and it was at this time that a pig club was founded in the village. Most families kept a pig, which provided meat for many families, and the pig club was only wound up in 1964.

The ten cottages in Upper Harlestone were built of brick in 1864. They replaced decayed freehold cottages and were a great improvement on earlier accommodation. They had in addition convenient allotments, at the end of each of which was accommodation for that pig! The population varied very little. The census of 1831 shows 563 people living in 94 houses, and in 1891 569 people in 134 houses. The high point was 1841 with 651 inhabitants.

St. Andrew's Church had been sadly neglected, and the incumbent, David Morton, who had been appointed in 1831 by Earl Spencer, started a major restoration programme. Sir George Gilbert Scott was engaged to restore and renovate the structure. First, drainage all round the church was improved, so that 'the green slime and dripping walls' of former days were no longer to be seen. The East Window, which had been, according to David Morton, "quasi-domestic in character" was replaced by the present window in Perpendicular style in 1837. Some of the renovations were less helpful. The quite elegant sedilia of Henry de Bray's church were 'improved' with the addition of some heavy carving, but fortunately most of the repairs were in the nature of improving drainage, and repairing stonework.. For Queen Victoria's Diamond Jubilee in 1897 the clear glass of the East Window was replaced with stained glass on the subject of Christ the King. At this point the chancel floor and arch were raised, to allow the window to be seen. Raising the arch created the crack above it which has the appearance of a roof line. The details of the window are interesting today, because they reflect Victoria's status as Empress of India, as well as Sovereign of the British Isles. They show the Patron Saints of the British Isles, and also St. Thomas for India, and the lotus flower as well as the rose, leek and shamrock. The first organ was installed in 1867, and the stone pulpit was replaced by the present one by a gift from the Duchess of Grafton in 1898. It incorporates fine Flemish carving dating from the sixteenth century, and the Duchess was assured by the antique dealer who supplied it that it had come originally from Fotheringhay Castle.

A new departure was the engineering works which Thomas Cooch opened at Manor Farm. The Cooch family had been tenants of Manor farm since 1710, and were related by marriage to the Camfield family. They were also notable inventors, and active in agricultural affairs.

Mr. Thomas Cooch was a founder member of Lamport Agricultural Society in 1797, and in the nineteenth century Joshua Cooch won first prize for a machine for dressing corn at all the shows where it was entered. He also produced various other agricultural machines, which were manufactured first at Manor Farm, where the brick buildings still stand, and later in Commercial Street, Northampton. The last Cooch to live in Manor Farm was Donald Cooch who died in 2009 at the age of 96.

Another manufacturing activity new to the village was a brick works in Upper Harlestone, whch produced the bricks used in the new buildings of the Ten Cottages in Upper Harlestone, and many other local buildings. On the other hand when many stone cottages fell into disrepair they were simply allowed to fall down. For most of the century agriculture was very depressed.

The increasing number of the poor placed burdens on parishes all over the country. In 1834 a Union for Poor Law Administration was formed. Harlestone was in the Brixworth Union of thirty six parishes, and a proper workhouse was formed. This workhouse has now been converted into a number of comfortable houses. The corner where this group stands is still known locally as Workhouse Bank. When Canon Bury, Rector of Harlestone, was in charge, his criteria for admission were so strict that he was known as "buryall". He held by three principles: Poor Law Relief was for the destitute and not for the deserving, the condition of the relieved person should be below that of the independent labourer, and the obligation to relieve lay primarily with the families and relatives of the indigent person. This made him unpopular and there was a strong reaction against him, although he was personally generous

By the end of that century, there were in the village 3 shops, plus a butcher and a baker. There were several small businesses – agricultural machinery, a mineral water manufacturer, a blacksmith and a miller, two regular carriers to Northampton, and also a variety of public servants – schoolmaster, constable, sub-postmaster, parish clerk, and of course the rector, and the curate. Contact with Northampton was increasingly easy, so more business was done in the market there, the carriers providing the necessary links. In 1890 William Spring, with the assistance of the Duchess of Grafton, opened the Dovecote Laundry. The bakehouse, which served all the people who had no ovens in their kitchens, was at first in Upper Harlestone, but in the 1870s a new bakehouse was built for Joseph Smeeton when he moved to the farmhouse "adjoining the turnpike" and the buildings opposite were used for the bake house and old bake house demolished. The village also had a Post Office.

During the 1830s letters were received at a house in Lower Harlestone, but the business then removed in 1840 to a newly built house in the middle of village, from which it has only recently been removed. The Post Office was also an off-license.

Farming was still the chief occupation. There were still six large farms – Manor Farm, Church Farm, Rock Farm, Yew Tree Farm, Park Farm, and Cross Hill Farm, and of course the Glebe farm. But the writing was on the wall. Many small farmers combined two jobs – farmer and machinist, painter and farmer, farmer and malster, grocer and draper, baker and farmer, butcher and grazier, surveyor and farmer, and a malster who was also a grazier, registrar, and assessor.

Extreme weather conditions occasionally occurred. In 1848 a violent hailstorm with hailstones up to three inches across hit the village, breaking the glass in the Orangery of Harlestone House, and in 1891 there was snow six inches deep on Whitsunday night.

Communication with the wider world became easier when first the canal systems, and then railways were developed. Neither system came through Harlestone, but the Grand Union Canal is not far away, and the railway from Northampton to Rugby, constructed in the nineteenth century, had a special station to serve Althorp. This station lies close to the Brampton Road, where several railway houses bear witness to the work this provided on the line. The construction involved many navvies from Ireland, who were famous for their hard work and play, being notorious drunkards. They lived in rough camps near the Brampton Brook, and even today it is still possible to find round bottomed bottles in which liquor – both hard and soft – was supplied in the nineteenth century. They were not allowed into the pubs, because they were so drunken and riotous, but went to drink at a "hole-in-the-wall" run by a man called Fisher. The Hole in the Wall on Fisher's Hill (also known as Windmill Hill) started in 1861, and continued until 1874. William Fisher died in 1882. Windmill Hill is named after a windmill, mentioned in Henry de Bray's Estate Book, which was until the last century near this hill.

Horses often had difficulty in drawing heavy loads up this hill, so when his countess died in 1903 Earl Spencer placed a memorial to her at the foot of the hill. The internal combustion engine has made this obsolete, but it still stands as a remembrance of earlier times.

There were many other drinking places. The Northampton Mercury on the 9th of July, 1759 referred to a meeting at the Bell, Harleston, but this is the only known reference to this pub, and it does not seem to have survived into the nineteenth century. On the other hand, a cottage in Upper Harlestone is known to have been a beer house called locally the Hole in the Wall. It had a fine beer cellar built into the hillside.

More enduring was the Fox and Hounds in Lower Harlestone. From 1887 - 1896 it was run as a co-operative. The Vicar was Chairman but like all the other cooperative ventures it reverted to private ownership.

Dovecote House in Upper Harlestone was also a pub called the Hare and Hounds, and in 1829 the licensee was John Lumley. For many years on St. Luke's Day, October 18, Harlestone Feast was celebrated here. The schoolchildren got a holiday and booths and roundabouts were set up in Chinkwell Lane. A fiddler played for dancing at the Hare and Hounds. The feast moved to New Duston when the Hare and Hounds stopped being a public house in the 1860s. It was converted into a private house in 1989.

As well as keeping a the Hare and Hounds, John Lumley was also a farmer, but was not good at either occupation, and lost his money. He worked for a few years as a gardener for the then rector, Canon Bury, and then went to be licensee of the Fox and Hounds in Lower Harlestone. After his death his widow, Mrs. Eliza Lumley, moved to a cottage in Cooch's Lane, where she had a Dame School for a while. She died in 1895, and for the first time in 600 years, the name Lumley disappeared from the village. There are no memorials to the early Lumleys, but the later family is commemorated, apart from headstones in the churchyard, and memorial plaques inside the church, by the two brass vases on the High Altar, which were given in 1971 in memory of Eric Lumley Edens.

The school remained an important part of the village, and grew and flourished. Stock was bought and invested by the Charity Commissioners. The charity continued to support the school, generally paying £30 a year to the schoolmaster, even after a National Society for Promoting the Education of the Poor had been established in 1811. For many years it is described as 'a National school, partly supported by an endowment and partly by the fees of the children'.

In 1808 Mr Cooch, from Manor Farm, had the floor in the old school relaid, and matchboard lining put on the walls at a cost of c. £30. Other repairs were carried out by Harlestone Charities in 1843 at a cost of £59. About 1840 these premises were converted into three cottages, which were let at a rent of £3 p.a. per cottage. A new school was built in 1840 on the site of outhouses which had belonged to the Lumley family, the schoolmaster's house adjoining having been the residence of Thomas Lumley in 1766. The acre of orchard attached was sold in 1840. The first schoolroom later became the part devoted to infants. About 1870 a classroom was added, and on the same site a larger schoolroom was built and opened in September, 1844. This was while the Revd. Canon Bury was rector. He drew up the plans with the help of Lord Spencer. There were at that time 188 pupils in the school, but the average attendance was 117. The schoolmaster lived in a house attached to the school building. When Joseph Fieldsend became headmaster in 1886, the schoolmaster's house was altered because there was only one room downstairs, and the same upstairs, with no back way or yard at all. It was during Canon Bury's time that the school was transferred from the Trustees of the National Society to the County Education Department.

The school before the fire with its thatched roof

For many years the school also had a Sunday School for children from the age of six, There was an average of 100 children in the regular school, and about 70 in the Sunday school, which was open from half past nine in the morning until half past one in the afternoon. The rules for the behaviour were strict. Children were to attend 'washed, combed and clean'. If they missed two Sundays without sufficient excuse, they would be excluded. Children who were seen to 'laugh, talk or behave otherwise improperly' in the class were to be punished. One has to wonder how strict discipline was in the regular school, if such standards were expected in a Sunday School!

Unfortunately many of the records of the nineteenth century school were destroyed in a fire in 1978, but from those few which survive, a picture of the type of education offered can be formed. Heavy emphasis was placed on fitting children for useful work. Basic skills were insisted on, with clear handwriting being particularly prized, and the school garden was well cultivated. Most of the boys leaving went simply into 'work', with agricultural work being sometimes specified, and the girls went into service, or simply to help at home. At that time most employment was on the land or in the great country houses. Harlestone House and Althorp were major employers, Althorp at one time having more than 100 gardeners. By the end of the century a few children were going on to education after the age of 14, to Northampton Grammar School or to technical schools – even, for girls, Dressmaking College, and the study of Domestic Economy became available.

All was not hard work, however. On one occasion after a lesson on the Gunpowder Plot, two tar barrels were set alight in the school garden, one must assume as a dramatic re-enaction of the consequences of an explosion!

The fire in 1978 destroyed not only the records of the early years, but the last thatched school in Northamptonshire. The new school was built in a similar style but with many improvements, and still flourishes.

Law and order continued to be enforced by the village constable until the creation of a professional police force, first with Sir Robert Peel's London 'bobbies' in 1829, and then the creation of a County Constabulary in 1839. Attempts were made locally to control crime through the establishment of the Harlestone Association for the Prosecution of Felons. This was one of the richest of similar societies of gentry, clergy and farmers because of the Spencer involvement. They could afford more flamboyant posters and bigger rewards. Members were led by Earl Spencer and included Robert Andrew, Mary Lumley, Henry Sanders, Charles Whiting and Thomas Warton. In 1802 at a meeting in the Fox and Hounds they '…resolved to procure a number of bloodhounds for the purpose of tracing and detecting sheep stealers'. These hounds successfully traced a man who had stolen a lamb, and he was hanged at the Assizes in Northampton for his crime.

In 1806 William Miles was charged with stealing a pair of 'patent cord breeches' from Robert Andrew of Harlestone Park, and in 1837 Edward Baker was charged with stealing various silver items from John Flavell, to the value of £3. 18s., incurring for this crime the death penalty.

The Baptist Chapel

Dissent has a long history in the village. The religious census of the province of Canterbury conducted in 1676 by Bishop Compton lists seven nonconformists for Harlestone, in contrast with none in Brington, and three in Brampton. There were at the same time 450 conformists, but no papists! In the Parish records, the daughter of John & Mary Wills is entered in 1715 as 'not baptized according to the rites

The Baptist Chapel Harlestone

of the Church of England', and the child of Anthony Cave in 1721 as 'not Christian burial' – possibly both of dissenting families. In 1740 Tubalcain York is listed as 'mason and Quaker buried at Bugbrooke'. Bugbrooke had a prominent Quaker meeting. In that same census of Bishop Compton there were 100 nonconformists there, and 300 who conformed.

Charles Wesley preached here on three occasions - 1769, 1770 and 1771. In his account of the 1779 visit he wrote: 'I preached at Alston (as it was pronounced locally) in a large malting room, where one side of my head was very warm through the crowd of people, and the other very cold, having an open window at my ear'. The village name first appeared in the local Methodist records in 1832, when three members formed a Methodist class. At one time there was a class of eighteen people, led by Nicholas Smith. One of Nicholas Smith's grandsons became a Mormon and moved to Salt Lake City in 1882. The village disappeared from the Circuit Plan in 1846, by which time the Baptists had taken over as the main dissenting sect.

Dr. John Ryland, a prominent Baptist minister in Northampton, preached in the village in 1775, and from then on Baptists became prominent in the village. At first they met in an outhouse lent by the Andrew family, where they also held a Sunday School. Then a barn belonging to a Mrs. Harris was converted into a meeting house. It became an official chapel in 1830, and was often referred to as 'the 1830 chapel'. This building was in Lower Harlestone, on Mill Lane, with access to the part of the brook known as Washbrook, which was used for immersion baptisms. On the opening day of this chapel, three sermons were preached on one day, by distinguished divines. When the new chapel was built in 1873, most of the old chapel was pulled down, and the remainder was merged with a house which is still there, adjacent to the pavement and between 'The Old House' and Mill Lane. On part of the old chapel is the inscription IME 1722. There are three families with a name beginning with 'E' recorded in the parish registers about this time – England, Errington and Edmunds, but none of them has the appropriate initials.

In 1873 a new chapel was opened on land given by the Fifth Earl Spencer. Since he was at that time Viceroy of Ireland, the deeds for the chapel were signed in Dublin Castle. The building could hold 150 people, and its main stones were donated by Mr Samuel Golby, a quarry manager in New Duston. His letter states: 'My workmen will give the labour'.

The building was 24' x 34' built of rock-faced masonry with dressed stone around the doorway and windows, with an entrance door in the North wall. Above the door was a canopied niche in which stood a sculpted figure of the Saviour, which had been given by a Mr. Welch. When the chapel was closed, the statue went to the headquarters in the town, presumably the Baptist Meeting, College Street, Northampton. A number of baptisms, with the name variously spelled Welsh, Welch, and Weltch, are recorded between 1616 and 1754, and several marriages between 1714 and 1735, but no burials. There is anecdotal evidence of a burial ground somewhere behind Park Farm House, but there is no documentary evidence.

In 1891 an extension consisting of schoolroom, kitchen and lavatories was built. In addition to Sunday School, the classroom was used for other social activities, because the Harlestone Institute was not opened until 1924. Music was provided by a harmonium played by Sally Marriot, a well known local character who had a small shop in what is now Virginia Cottage, with Mrs Dickins, whose descendents later lived in the former chapel, as first reserve. Magic Lantern slide shows on topics such as missionaries and animals were regularly given. The Magic Lantern, which was originally candle operated, was later converted to electricity and transferred to the Institute. It was an exhibit in the Daventry Museum, till that museum was closed.

The Superintendent of the Sunday School, amongst other activities, arranged an annual outing to Althorp, where tea was provided and parties came from other chapels. They travelled in horse drawn wagons and apparently had a very enjoyable day. Occasionally the trips were more adventurous, for example taking the train to Skegness or Hunstanton.

The nineteenth century came to an end with a flourish. Queen Victoria's Diamond Jubilee was celebrated in style. The event was celebrated in the church with a stained glass window on the theme of Christ in glory surrounded by Royal Saints. A cedar tree was planted in the churchyard and a horse chestnut in Upper Harlestone. The horse chestnut remains but the cedar tree fell down in 1998.

In spite of the difficult times in agriculture, there was optimism as the new century began. The Empire was at its height, and people looked forward to peace and prosperity in the twentieth century.

8   LOOSE ENDS

The last tenant of Harlestone House, the Duchess of Grafton, lived there until her death in 1928. Her death was the end, not just of Harlestone House, but of a whole era. She was the last Lady Bountiful in the old style, giving very generously to the village, as she thought best. No child in her time went to school without shoes, children with good school reports were rewarded with lengths of material for new clothes, every new baby got a gift usually of material for clothes or some other useful contribution. Every Empire Day she gave a party for the whole village which was still remembered with nostalgic enjoyment by elderly villagers almost a century later. She helped generously the families of men wounded or killed in the Great War, and assisted those wishing to emigrate to Canada or the colonies.

One of the many contributions she made to the village was in starting a fund to build the Village Institute. In 1883 Canon William Bury, the Rector, first mentioned the need for a room for readings and other meetings, to replace the room in a beer house on Fisher's Hill (now called Windmill Hill on the A428 in Lower Harlestone) at that time used as a parish hall. But it was in 1898 that the Duchess started a fund to build a village hall, with a donation of £80. The Institute was eventually built in 1924.

After her death the Harlestone House was left untenanted for more than eleven years, and fell into disrepair. In 1940 it was sold to demolition contractors, and pulled down. The site and the ruins were a favourite playground for village children, and it was used for the storage of agricultural machinery during World War II. Only the gardens and stables remained, and the grandiose stables are still standing, now converted into houses. The site was sold in 1990 by Earl Spencer to Northampton Golf Club, and their Clubhouse stands today overlooking the lake.

When the Baptist Chapel closed as a place of worship, it was sometimes used for other activities, by organisations such as Boy Scouts, the Home Guard and the Boys Brigade. However, it became disused again in the late 1940s. In early June 1950 Mr. and Mrs. Dickins, whose father had been involved with the original building, and who had also been superintendent of the Sunday School, applied for planning permission to convert it into a home. It is today a delightful house, with wonderful views to Althorp and to the village – in fact, one of the first of the conversions of village properties which became more common in later years.

Manor Farm remained until 2009 in the hands of the Cooch family. The brick buildings which are today part of the farmyard are relics of their manufacturing activities. The inventive strain continued into the twentieth century, when Mr. H. Cooch, RFC, invented a device for landing aircraft in fog while at the Royal Aircraft Establishment, Farnborough. The stained glass window at the west end of the

Vera Low's cottage in 1978

Vera Low's cottage 2008

south aisle is in memory of Annie Cooch, who died in 1901.

In the 1980s, the Spencers sold off the freeholds to many cottages, which were becoming very dilapidated, and were being abandoned as agriculture became more mechanised, and many fewer people were employed on the farms. They were bought by incomers, who spent large sums of money putting in damp courses, and bringing the accommodation up to modern standards. Since many of the cottages had gardens around them, once used for producing vegetables for their occupants use, there was scope for extension, especially when outbuildings like pigstyes were included. The results were sometimes astonishing.

The close knit community of the past is gone and a new life will no doubt evolve as the years pass. There was much that was good in the old communities, but not everything. There was a lot of illness – TB and smallpox were recurring scourges, and the life was extremely hard with laborious, outside work in all weathers. Young people today would not be prepared to walk four miles to Northampton for entertainment, nor be content with church youth clubs, and village socials. The communication revolution has brought a new dimension into village life.

Two world wars, the mechanisation of agriculture, improvements in communication, and all the pressures of the modern world, have changed the village from an agricultural community with a strong local loyalty, and it has not yet at the beginning of the twentieth first century developed a new ethos. The history of the twentieth century is the story of this loss of history and gain in living standards. It will be interesting to see what the future holds.

INDEX

A

Act, Enclosure of 1767 52, 56
Advowson 14, 27, 35, 36, 39
Alston 7, 75
Althorp 11, 21, 39, 40, 43, 63, 65, 67, 69, 72, 74
Andrew Family 39, 44, 51, 56, 58, 73
Andrew, Gilbert 56
Andrew, John, 62
Andrew, Robert 31, 38, 43, 44, 45, 47, 53, 54, 56, 62, 63, 72
Andrew, Sir Thomas 45
Andrew, Thomas 21, 32, 43, 44, 45
Anglo-Saxon 9, 12, 23
Archbold, Sir Nicholas 34
Armenters, Brixtan de 14
Austen, Jane 50

B

Bannaventa 8, 10
Barrington, Viscount 61
Bewe, le 19
Black Death 31
Blore, Edward 64
Book, Domesday 11, 12, 19, 24
Brampton 7, 13, 21, 32, 42, 53
Brampton, Chapel 39
Braunston 44
Bridge, Clapper 10
Brington 7, 12, 23, 39, 40, 43
Brington, Great 8, 40, 59
Brockhall 22
Brook, Brampton 5, 56, 65, 69
Brook, Harlestone 5, 7, 28, 56

Buckby, Long 39, 42, 59
Bugbrooke 73
Bulmer (Bolymer) 22, 31, 61
Bury, Canon William 68, 70, 77

C

Callis, Simon 56
Camfields (Calmfields) 42, 44
Canal, Grand Union 69
Canons, Augustinian 13
Carleton, John Pykard de 22
Carr, Robert 43
Cart, Richard 37
Castle, Fotheringhay 45, 67
Castle, Lumley 21
Catuvellauni 8
Cavalier, Revd. H.O. 8, 9
Cave, Anthony 73
Chapel, The Baptist 73, 74, 77
Church, St. Andrew's 14, 23, 27, 34, 35, 39 42, 61, 64, 65, 67,
Clare, John 57
Clark, George of Scaldwell 54
Clendon, John 52, 53
Clinton, Edward Lord 35
Club, Jockey 65
Club, Northampton Golf 77
Cocks, Elizabeth 35
College, Gresham 7
College, Yale 42
Colonel Fairfax 39
Common Prayer, Book of 39
Compton, Bishop 72
Confessor, Edward the 12
Connecticut, Charter of 42
Constabulary, County 72
Cooch, Annie 79
Cooch, Joshua 68
Cooch, Thomas 56, 68
Cooperative Dairy Assoc'

65
Corn Laws 67
Cotherstone 65
Cottages, Ten 68, 67
Cottage, Virginia 74
Cromwell, Oliver 45, 46
Cross, James 59
Cross, Richard 58
Crusade, First 13

D

Dallington, Prior of 14
Danelaw 11
Daventry 8, 10, 39, 44
de Bray 13, 19, 27, 37, 39
de Bray, Henry 14, 23, 25, 28, 31
De Het(te), Richard 23
Dent Family 58
Derby, Earls of 14, 40
Dickins, Family 74
Doddridge, Dr. Charles 40
Dunchurch 42, 43, 52
Dunkley, George 65
Durham, County 21

Duston 8, 10, 11, 12, 31
Duston, New 43, 70, 74
Dyve Family 21, 22, 23, 24, 32, 61
Dyve, Sir Lewis 31, 39

E

Edens, Eric Lumley 70
Edgeworth, Richard Lovell 61
Edric 12
Edward II 25
Edward III 22
Edward VI 34, 35
Elizabeth I 35
El Mansoor, Khalif 13
Empire Day 77
England, Arthur 51
England, Church of 73
England, Elizabeth 43
England, John 38
England, Richard 38, 51

80

Estate, Lumley 19
Estate, Spencer 64
Exhibition, Great 64

F

Farms
    Church 10, 34, 69
    Cross Hill 69
    Fleetland 56
    Glebe 34, 56, 69
    Manor 14, 19, 21, 32, 33,
        44, 68, 69, 70, 77
    Mill 56
    Park 8, 34, 69
    Rock 34, 58, 69
    Yew Tree 34, 65, 69
Fawsley 12, 34
Feast, Harlestone 70
Felons, Assoc for the Pros-
    ecution of 72
Field, Playing 65
Fieldsend, Joseph 70
Fire, Great of Northamp-
    ton 61
Fisher 38
Fisher, William 69
Flavell, John 72
Frankpledge 27

G

Gealing, Richard 55
Gealing, Thomas 43
Gifford, Richard 27
Gitda 12
Glazun, Robert 14
Golby, Samuel 74
Grafton, Duchess of 65,
    67, 68, 77
Gregory(s) 44, 53
Gregory, Thomas 36
Gregory, Valentine 35, 36,
    38, 39
Gregory, William 36
Grindale 23
Gross, Joseph 56
Grove, Newbottle 38
Guineas, 2000 65

H

Haddon, East 40
Halifax, Earl of 40
Halston 7, 55
Hanbury, William 58
Hanwell, Mr. 59
Harlestone 5, 10, 11, 12,
    13, 14, 17, 19, 20,
    21, 22, 23, 25, 27,
    28, 31, 32, 33, 35,
    38, 39, 42, 44, 45,
    52, 54, 56, 57, 59,
    61, 63, 64, 65, 68,
    69, 72
Harlestone, (Lord of) the
    Manor of 61
Harlestone, Lower 19, 46,
    52, 65, 69, 73, 77
Harlestone, Rector of 68
Harlestone, Upper 10, 19,
    32, 34, 36, 40, 43,
    56, 65, 67, 68, 69,
    70, 75
Harpole 8, 34, 36
Harris, Agnes 38
Harris, Richard 38
Harris, Samuel 58
Harris, Thomas 58
Heath, Dives 8, 21
Heath, Harlestone 34, 40,
    41, 50
Heath, Poors 37
Helpston 57
Henry II 27, 34
Henry III 39
Henry VIII 34
Herolve 11
Hesilrigg, Sir Arthur 41
Heyford 22
Heyford, de 21
Highway, Overseers of
    the 49
Hill, Fisher's 69, 77
Hill, Hopping 34, 43
Hill, Windmill 21, 69, 77
Holdenby 39, 40
Holme, Whiting's 44
House, Cottesbrooke 50
House, Dovecote 21, 49, 70

House, Harlestone 49, 50,
    52, 62, 64, 65, 67,
    69, 72, 77
Hul, Old Milne 19
Hundred, Newbottle 43
Hundred, Nobottle Grove
    12, 23

I

Industrial Society Ltd 65
Institute, Harlestone Village
    74, 77
Ireland, Viceroy of 64, 74
Isabella, Queen 25
Isham, Sir Justinian 58

J

James II 61
James, Abbey of St. 13,
    23, 25
Jarman, Nicholas 37
Joyce, Cornet 40

K

Kerton Family 44
Kerton, Thomas 56
Keynes, de 21
Kislingbury 34, 40, 54
Knightley, Emma 44
Knightley, Richard 44
Knightleys of Fawsley 39
Knightly, William 58
Knight, Richard 38
Kynne, Nicholas 32

L

Lac, Agnes 26
Lack 38, 58
Lane, Chinkwell 70
Lane, Church 7, 50, 51
Lane, Cooch's 55, 70
Lane, Lake 44
Lane, Glebe 11
Lane, Mill 73
Laundry, Dovecote 68
Law, Poor 49, 68

81

Lenton, Priory of 14, 23, 25, 27, 34
Leuric 12
Lilbourne 12
Lincoln 35
Line 58
Lloyd, Martha 50
Lodge, Grafton 43
Lole, Valentine 38
London, Recorder of 61
Lovell, Baron Henry 61, 54
Lovell, Lady 62
Lovell, Rachel Jane 61
Lovell, Sir Salathiel 61
Lumley, John 70,
Lumley, Mary 72
Lumley, Mrs. Eliza 70
Lumleys (de), 19, 21, 22, 23, 24, 31, 32, 37, 44, 49 56
Lumley, Thomas 32, 49, 70
Lumley, Tubalcain 49

M

Magic Lantern 74
Manning 56
Manning, Richard 59
Manning, John 49
Map, Eyre's 51
Map, Ogilby's 42, 43
Massachusetts Bay Colony 42
Marriot, Sally 74
Maultings 65
Mercia, Kingdom of 11
Mercury, Northampton 58, 59, 69
Messager, Ralph 37
Mill, The 19
Monasteries, Dissolution of the 53
Morcar(kere) 12
Morley, Valentine 36, 39
Mormons 73
Mortain, Count of 12, 13, 19, 21
Morton, David 67
Morton's Natural History of Northampton 55

Morwick, Hugh de 21, 22
Mother Redcap's Well 32
Museum, British 9, 17
Museum, Daventry 74

N

Naseby 40
Nassington, Prebendal Manor 17
Nelson 38
Nene, River 5
Newmarket 65
Nonconformists 42, 72
Noon, Benjamin 51
Normans 12, 13, 19
Normandy, William of 12
Northampton 12, 13, 25, 27, 31, 35, 39, 42, 43, 47, 49, 52, 61, 68, 69, 73, 74
Northampton, Earl of 12
Northampton, Eyre of 27
Northamptonshire 5, 8, 11, 12, 17, 38, 57, 72
Northamptonshire, Baker's History of 7
Northamptonshire, High Sheriff of 45
Nottingham 14

O

Office, Northampton Record 50
Office, Post 7, 65, 68
Ogilby, John 42
Open Fields 26, 28
Orange, William of 61
Orgar 12

P

Packe, James 62
Packe, Colonel 63
Packe, Frances 45, 57
Paeda, King 10
Pain, Tom 53
Palace, Buckingham 64

Palace, Crystal 64
Palace, Vorontsov 64
Park, Harlestone 47, 49, 58, 62, 64, 72
Park, Hyde 64
Park, Mansfield 50
Parliament 39, 58
Parliamentarians 39
Peel, Sir Robert 72
Penda, King 10
Peterborough 11, 35, 57
Pettit, John 44
Peverel Manor 12
Pev(w)erel, William 13, 14, 23, 33
Pheasantry 50
Pig Club 67
Plague, Bubonic 11, 31
Plate, Spencer 41
Plot, Gunpowder 72
Poor, National Society for Promoting the Education of the 70
Poor, Overseers of the 49, 57
Prince Rupert 39
Protestantism 34
Public Houses
   Wall, Hole in the 69
   Hounds, Fox and 42, 52, 64, 65, 69
   Hounds, Hare and 70
Pulteney, Sir John 44
Puritans(ism) 34, 35, 42
Pykard, John de Carleton 22

Q

Quaker 73
Quarry, Halston 7
Quarries 32, 33, 34, 49, 58
Quena 14, 17, 84

R

Racecourse, Northampton 41
Ralf, Earl of Hereford 12
Rectory 54, 64
Reformation 14, 23, 39, 57
Relief, Poor Law 68
Repton Brothers 62
Repton, Humphrey 63
Revolution, Glorious 61
Rigby(bie), George 38
Roads
  Brampton 7, 56, 69
  Brington 7
  Duston 10
  New 52
  Port 10, 32, 43
  Roman 7
Robert, St. James's. 14
Romans 8, 10, 11, 34
Royalist 39
Rugby 69
Ryland, Dr. John 73

S

Saltwell 17, 32
Sanders, Henry 72
Sand, Northampton 34
Saxons, Middle 11
Scarborough, Earls of 21, 61
School, Harlestone 54
School, Northampton Grammar 72
School, Sunday 71, 74
Scots, Mary Queen of 45
Scott, Sir George Gilbert 67
Sebod, Robert 26
Senlis, Simon de 13
Shortgrave 53
Shortgrave, Reverend 7
Shortgrave, Richard 36
Shortgrave, Robert 36
Shortgrave, William 36, 39, 52
Shuckborough, Nether 54
Smeeton, Joseph 68

Smith 38
Smith, Nicholas 73
Smith, Thomas 59
Society, Cooperative 65
Society, Harpole Industrial and Provident 65
Society, Lamport Agricultural 68
Southam, James 59
Spencer, Captain the Honorable Frederick 65
Spencer, Earl 56, 64, 67, 72
Spencer, Lord 47, 58, 64, 70
Spencer, Sarah 65
Spencer, Sir John 45
Spencer, Sixth Earl 65
Spencer, William Lord 41
Spring, William 68
Stacey, John 57
Stakes, Althorp Park 41
Stakes, Derby 65
Stamp, Alice 42
Stanley, Isabella 38
Stanton, Edward 62
Stanton, Thomas 38
Starmer 56
Staunton, Hugh de 27
Staunton, William de 14
Staverton 44
St James, Abbey of 13, 23, 25
St Mary's 39
Stormer, John 33
-Street, Watling 8, 10, 12
Stud, Althorp 65
Suffolk, Lord 64

T

Tax, Hearth 43
Templars 25
Thenerchebray, Lord Ralph 19, 23
Touchstone 65
Townsend, Joseph 61
Townsend, Maria 62
Travell 38
Tresham, George 35
Turnpike 50, 52, 56

U

Union, Brixworth 68
University, Yale 42
Upton 12, 13
Upton, Manorial Court of 12

V

Victoria, Queen 12, 67, 64
Viking 12

W

Waltheof, Earl of Northampton 12
War, Civil 39, 40, 46
War, Great 77
Warren, John 65
War, Second Civil 40
War, World II 77
Warwickshire 54
Washbrook 74
Way, Dallington 32
Way, Holdenby 32
Way, King's 26
Welch(sh)(tch), Mr. 74
Wesley, Charles 73
West, Benjamin 56
West, John 26
Whetecroft, le 19
Whig 58
Whiting 38, 44, 56
Whitinge, Edward 44
Workhouse 58

APPENDIX 1 - THE DE BRAY FAMILY

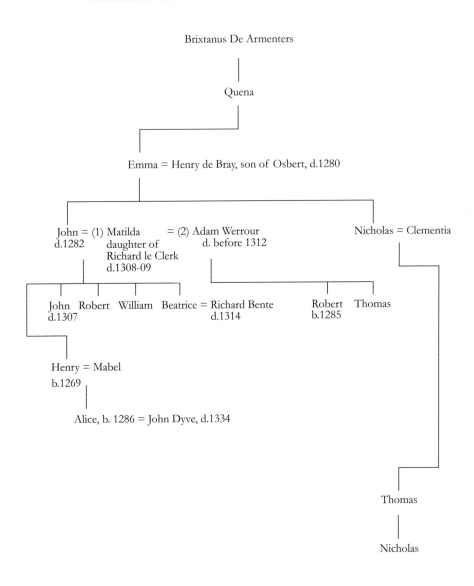

APPENDIX 2 - THE LUMLEY/BULMER FAMILIES

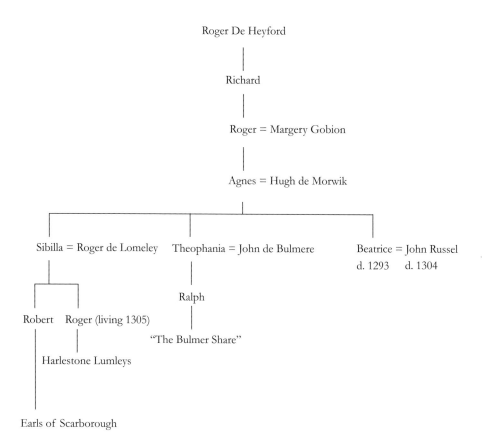

Roger De Heyford

Richard

Roger = Margery Gobion

Agnes = Hugh de Morwik

Sibilla = Roger de Lomeley   Theophania = John de Bulmere   Beatrice = John Russel
d. 1293   d. 1304

Robert   Roger (living 1305)   Ralph

"The Bulmer Share"

Harlestone Lumleys

Earls of Scarborough

APPENDIX 3 - THE CAMFIELD/COOCH CONNECTION

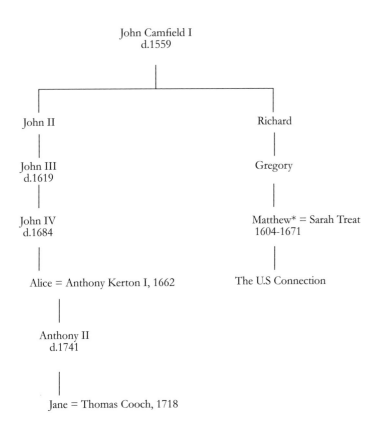

John Camfield I
d.1559

John II

John III
d.1619

John IV
d.1684

Alice = Anthony Kerton I, 1662

Anthony II
d.1741

Jane = Thomas Cooch, 1718

Richard

Gregory

Matthew* = Sarah Treat
1604-1671

The U.S Connection

*Emigrated to Massachusetts Bay Colony,
c.1630. Married daughter of the
Governor of New Jersey

CHIEF SOURCES

Northamptonshire Record Society
Public Record Office, Kew
Northamptonshire Record Office
    The Andrew Collection
    The Spencer Collection
    The Hughes Collection
    Harlestone Wills
Baker, G. *The History & Antiquities of the County of Northamptonshire* (Nichols & Son, London) 1822
Birmingham Public Reference Library *Indenture of covenants concerning the sale of Harlestone.* MS 242786
Bolton, J. L. *The Medieval English Economy* (J. M. Dent) 1985
Bridges, John *The History & Antiquities of the County of Northamptonshire* ed. P. Whalley 1791
Cavalier, The Revd. H. O. *The Roman Site at Sharoah near Nobottle*
Domesday Book Northamptonshire Philimore Press 1979
Douglas-Home, M. *A Spencer Childhood 1994*
Giggins, Brian *Northampton's Forgotten Castle* 1999
Greenall, R. *A History of Northamptonshire* Philimore Press 1979
Goff, J. *We Never could Say Their Name* 1975
Hall, D.N. *The Open Fields of Northamptonshire* 1995
Harvey, J.H. *English Medieval Architects* A Biographical Dictionary 1984
Maclean, Teresa *Medieval English Gardens* 1981
Morton, J. *Natural History of Northamptonshire* 1712
Pevsner, N. *Northamptonshire* 1981
Pryor F. *Farmers in Prehistoric Britain* 1999
Royal Commission on Historical Monuments *Archaeological sites in North-West Northamptonshire* 1981
Spencer, C. *The Spencers* St Martins Press 1999
Sutherland, D.S *Northamptonshire Stone* 2003
Sutherland, D.S *Northamptonshire Slatestones*
Taylor, C.C.. *Village and Farmstead* Dent 1983
Victoria County History Northampton
Wake, J. *English Historical Review* 1922
D. Willis ed. *The Estate Book of Henry de Bray* Camden Society 1913

ACKNOWLEDGEMENTS

Inhabitants of Harlestone, many alas no longer with us, including Mr. Donald Cooch, Mr. Robert Dickens, the Revd. Samuel Faulkner, Mrs. Elizabeth Smith and others living too numerous to name. My thanks also go to the staff at the Record Office, to Mr. Ron Greenall, Leicester University, Mark Andrew sand to Mrs. David McLean, (great granddaughter of Col Henry Packe) for information about the Mary Queen of Scots Jewel, and to the National Museum of Scotland for the photographs of that jewel. Special thanks to Ania Grzesik for her invaluable assistance with editing and printing this book.